FOR ORGANS, PIANOS & ELECTRONIC KEYBOARDS

E-Z PLAY TODAY 271

Favorite Christmas Songs

ISBN 0-634-08195-0

7777 W. BLUEMOUND RD. P.O. BOX 13819 MILWAUKEE, WI 53213

For all works contained herein:
Unauthorized copying, arranging, adapting, recording or public performance is an infringement of copyright.
Infringers are liable under the law.

E-Z PLAY® TODAY Music Notation © 1975 by HAL LEONARD CORPORATION

E-Z PLAY and EASY ELECTRONIC KEYBOARD MUSIC are registered trademarks of HAL LEONARD CORPORATION.

Visit Hal Leonard Online at
www.halleonard.com

CONTENTS

4	**Because It's Christmas (For All the Children)**
12	**Blue Christmas**
14	**Brazilian Sleigh Bells**
20	**C-H-R-I-S-T-M-A-S**
22	**Christmas Is**
24	**The Christmas Song (Chestnuts Roasting on an Open Fire)**
26	**Christmas Time Is Here**
9	**Do You Hear What I Hear**
28	**Feliz Navidad**
31	**Frosty the Snow Man**
34	**The Gift**
39	**Grandma Got Run Over by a Reindeer**
42	**Grown-Up Christmas List**
46	**Happy Christmas, Little Friend**
52	**Happy Holiday**
49	**Happy Xmas (War Is Over)**
57	**Hard Candy Christmas**
54	**Here Comes Santa Claus (Right Down Santa Claus Lane)**
60	**A Holly Jolly Christmas**
62	**(There's No Place Like) Home for the Holidays**
64	**I Saw Mommy Kissing Santa Claus**
66	**I Wish Everyday Could Be Like Christmas**
74	**I'll Be Home for Christmas**
76	**I've Got My Love to Keep Me Warm**
69	**It Must Have Been the Mistletoe (Our First Christmas)**
78	**It's Beginning to Look Like Christmas**
81	**Jingle-Bell Rock**
84	**Let It Snow! Let It Snow! Let It Snow!**
86	**Light of the Stable**
88	**Little Saint Nick**
90	**A Marshmallow World**
92	**Merry Christmas, Darling**
98	**Merry Christmas Waltz**
95	**The Night Before Christmas Song**
100	**Nuttin' for Christmas**
102	**Rudolph the Red-Nosed Reindeer**
105	**Silver Bells**
108	**Suzy Snowflake**
111	**This Christmas**
114	**Wonderful Christmastime**
119	***REGISTRATION GUIDE***

Because It's Christmas
(For All the Children)

Registration 2
Rhythm: Swing

Music by Barry Manilow
Lyric by Bruce Sussman and Jack Feldman

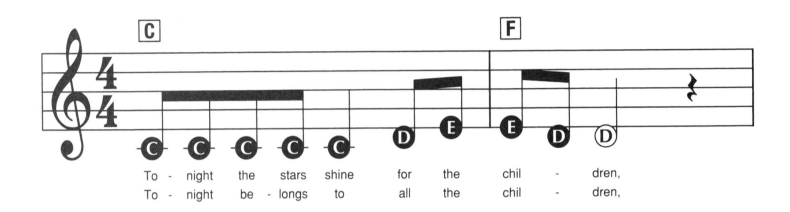

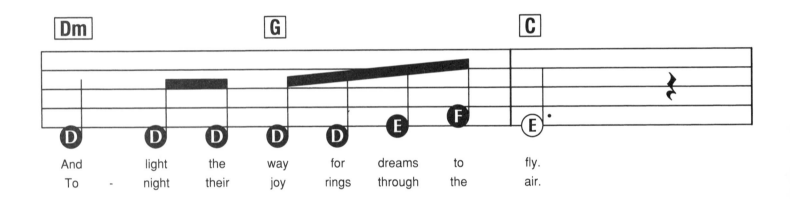

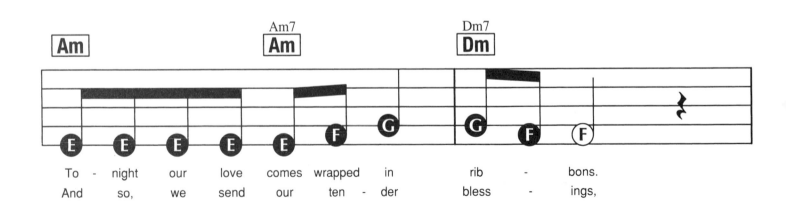

Copyright © 1986 by Careers-BMG Music Publishing, Inc., Appoggiatura Music and Camp Songs Music
All Rights Administered by Careers-BMG Music Publishing, Inc.
International Copyright Secured   All Rights Reserved

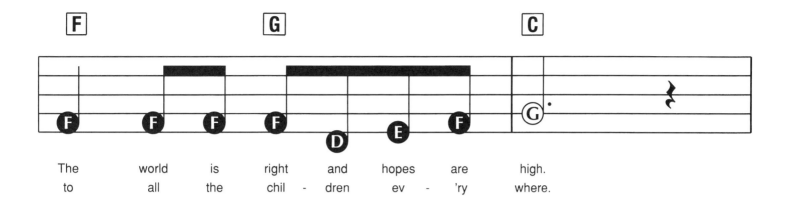
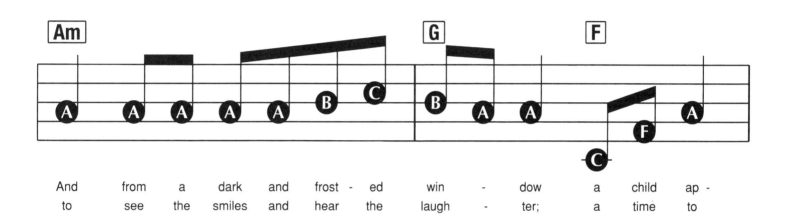
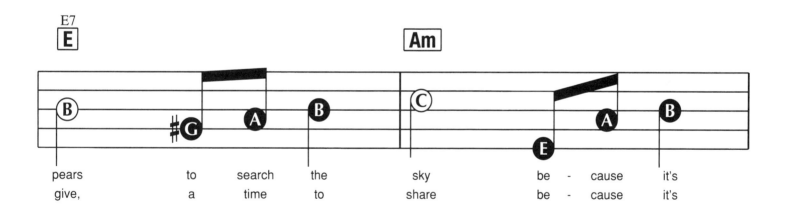
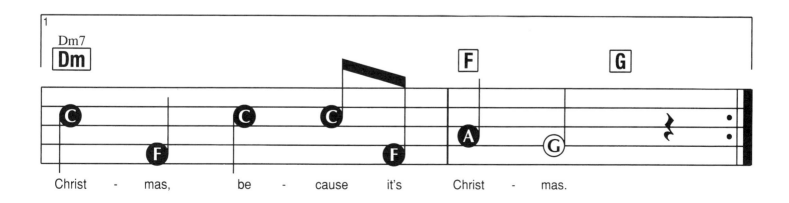

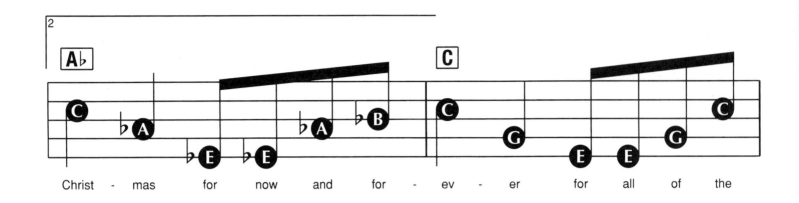
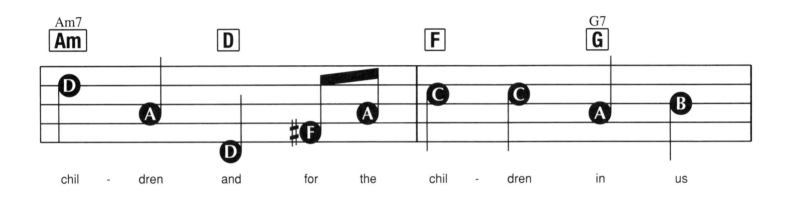
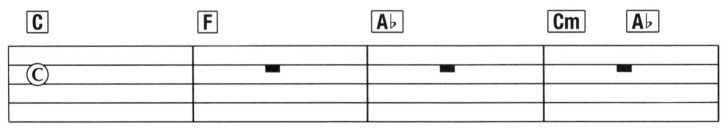
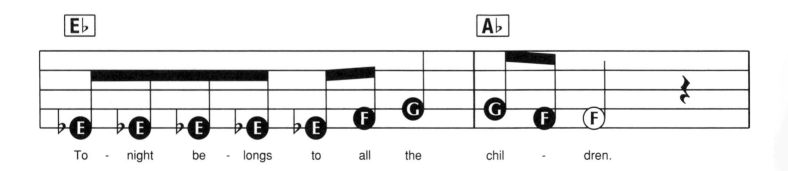

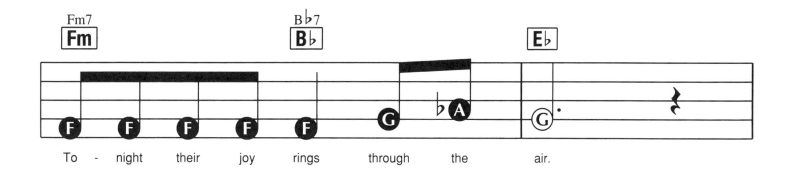
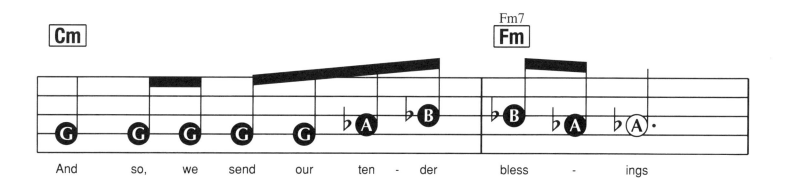
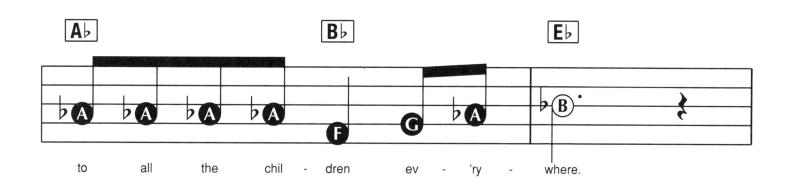
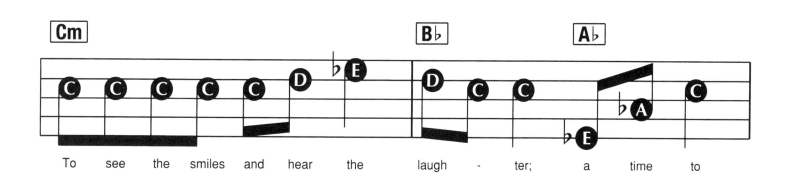

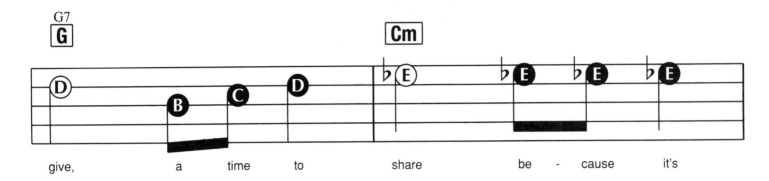
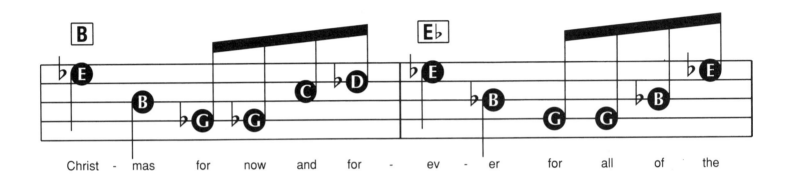
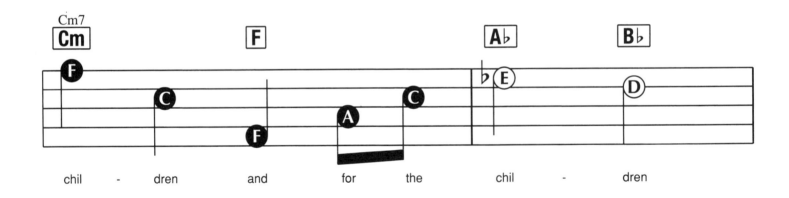
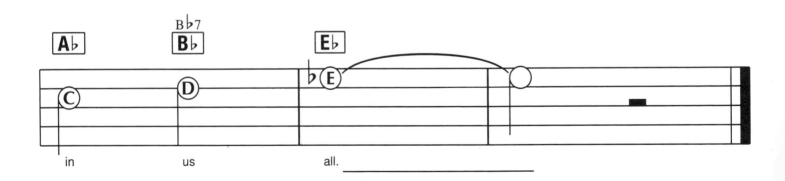

Do You Hear What I Hear

Registration 8
Rhythm: March

Words and Music by Noel Regney
and Gloria Shayne

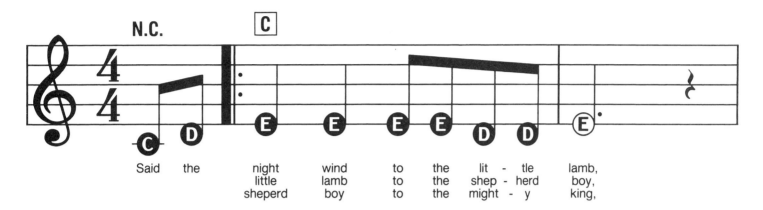

Said the night wind to the lit - tle lamb,
little lamb to the shep - herd boy,
sheperd boy to the might - y king,

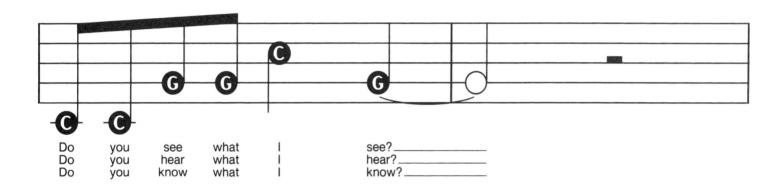

Do you see what I see?
Do you hear what I hear?
Do you know what I know?

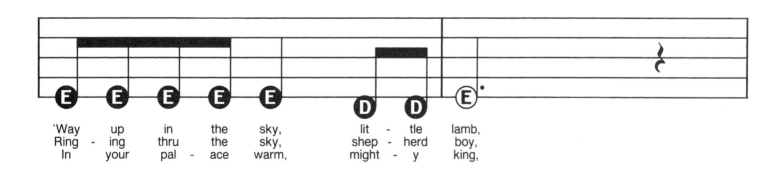

'Way up in the sky, lit - tle lamb,
Ring - ing thru the sky, shep - herd boy,
In your pal - ace warm, might - y king,

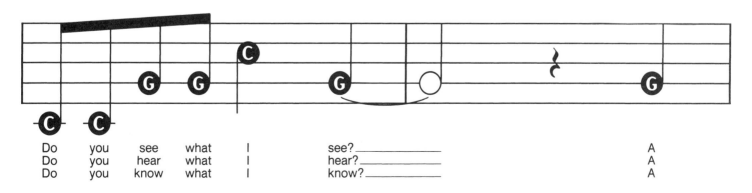

Do you see what I see? A
Do you hear what I hear? A
Do you know what I know? A

Copyright © 1962 by Regent Music Corporation (BMI)
Copyright Renewed by Jewel Music Publishing Co., Inc. (ASCAP)
International Copyright Secured All Rights Reserved
Used by Permission

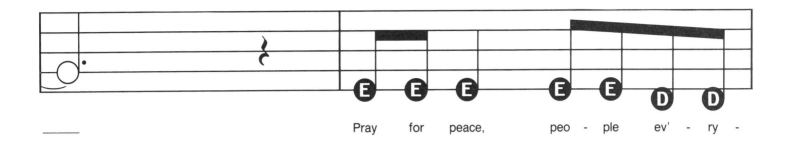
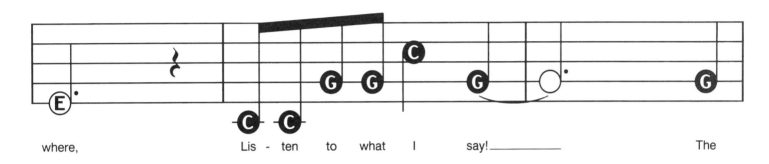
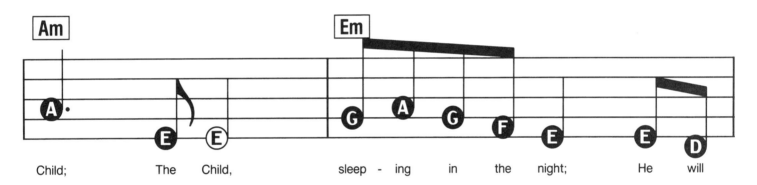
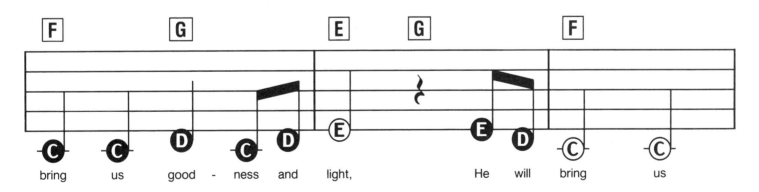
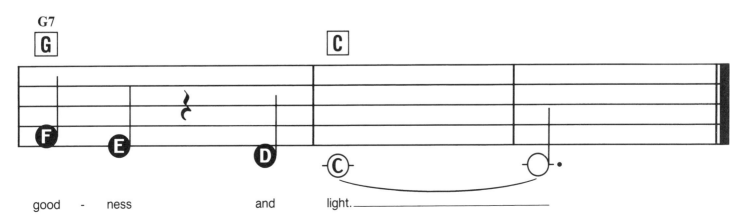

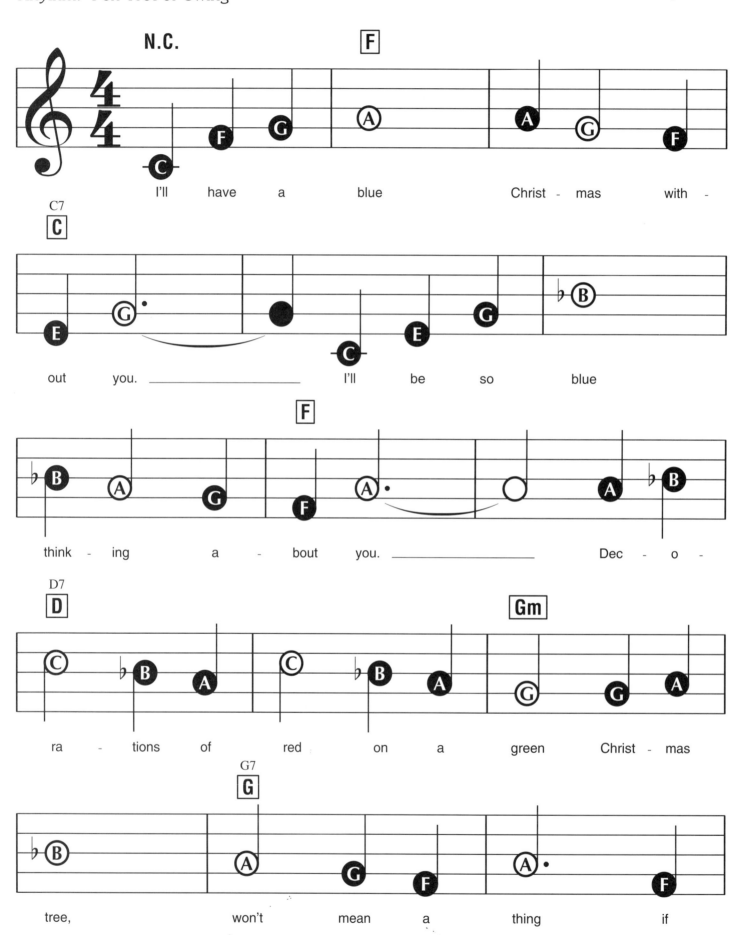

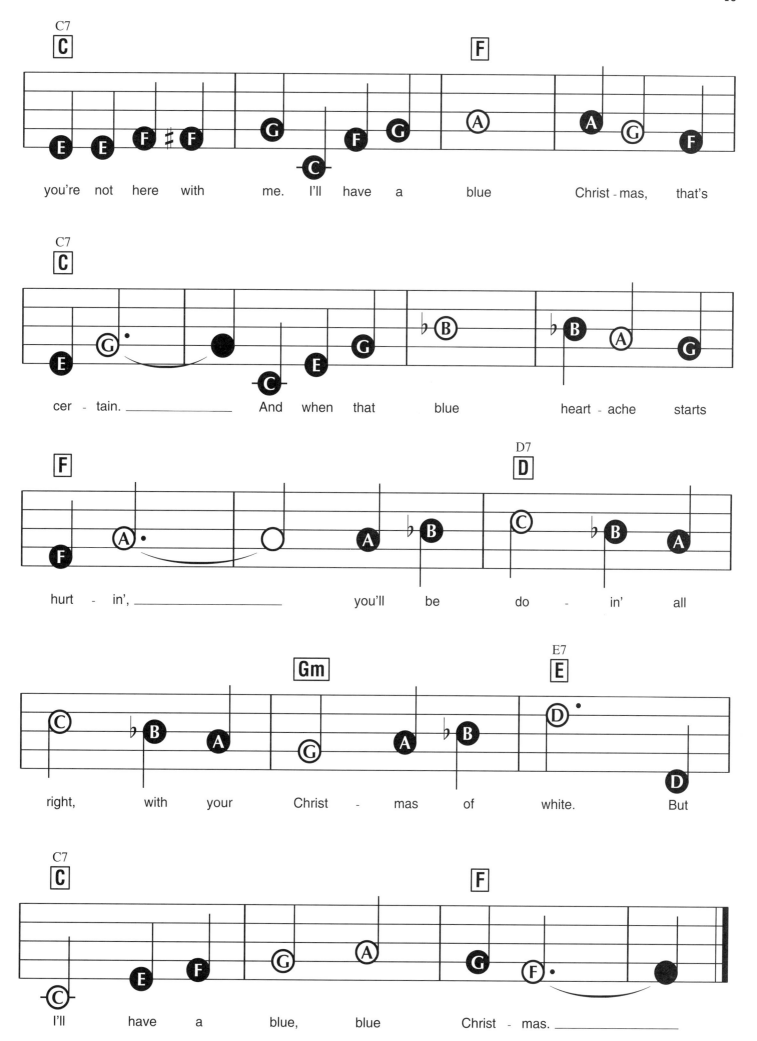

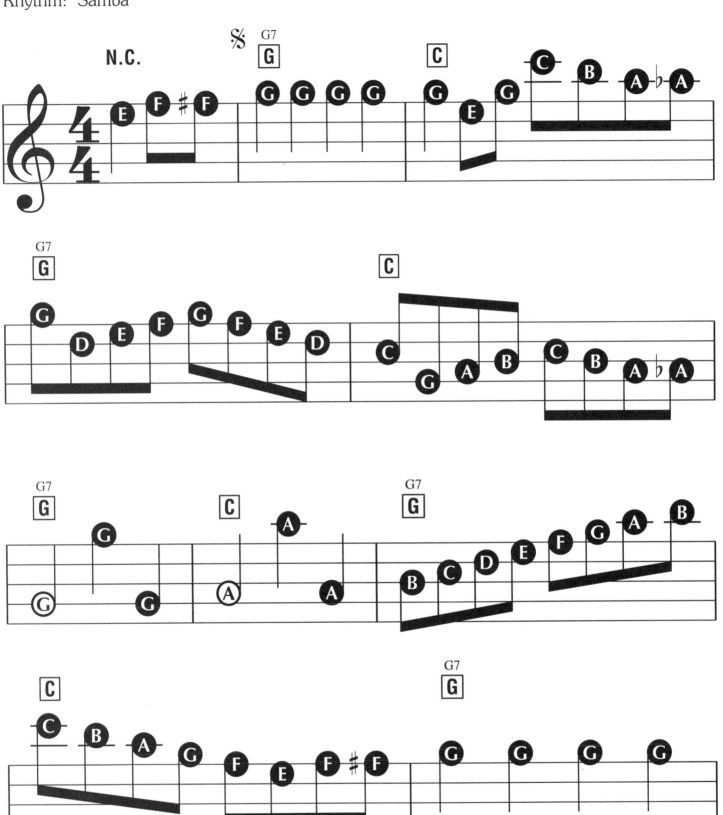

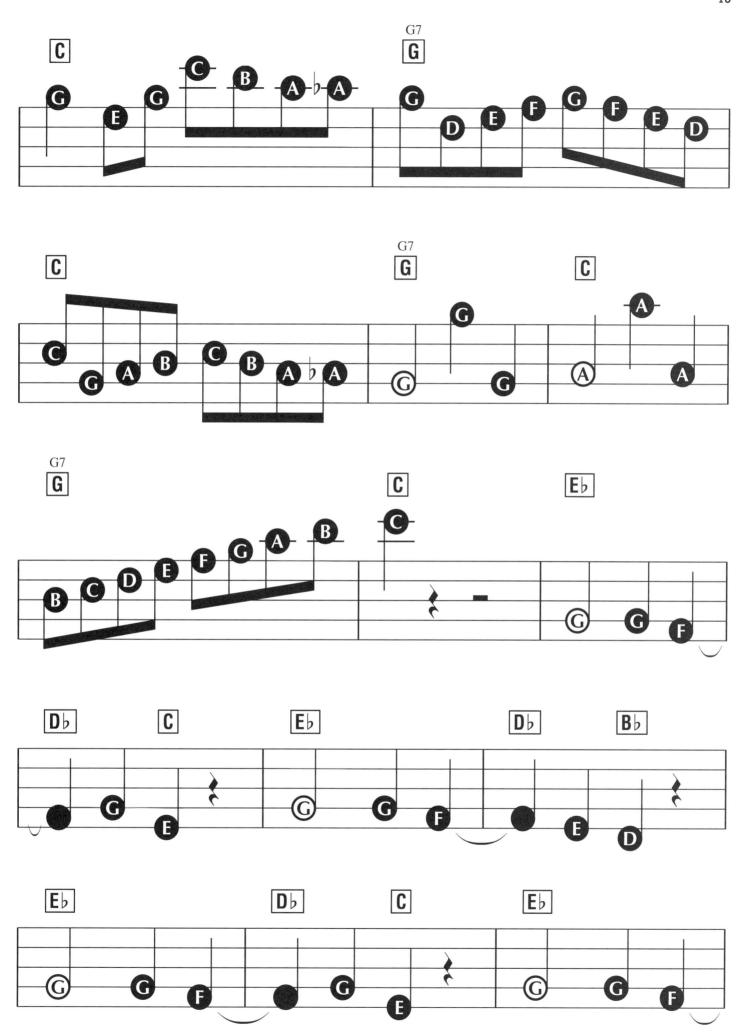

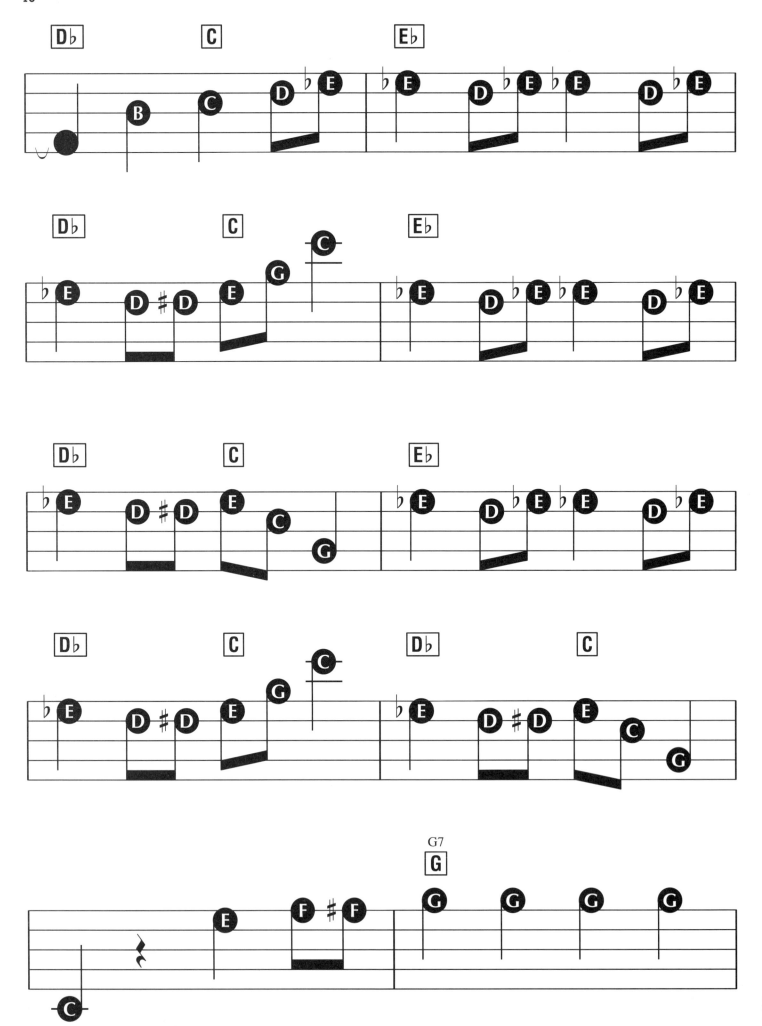

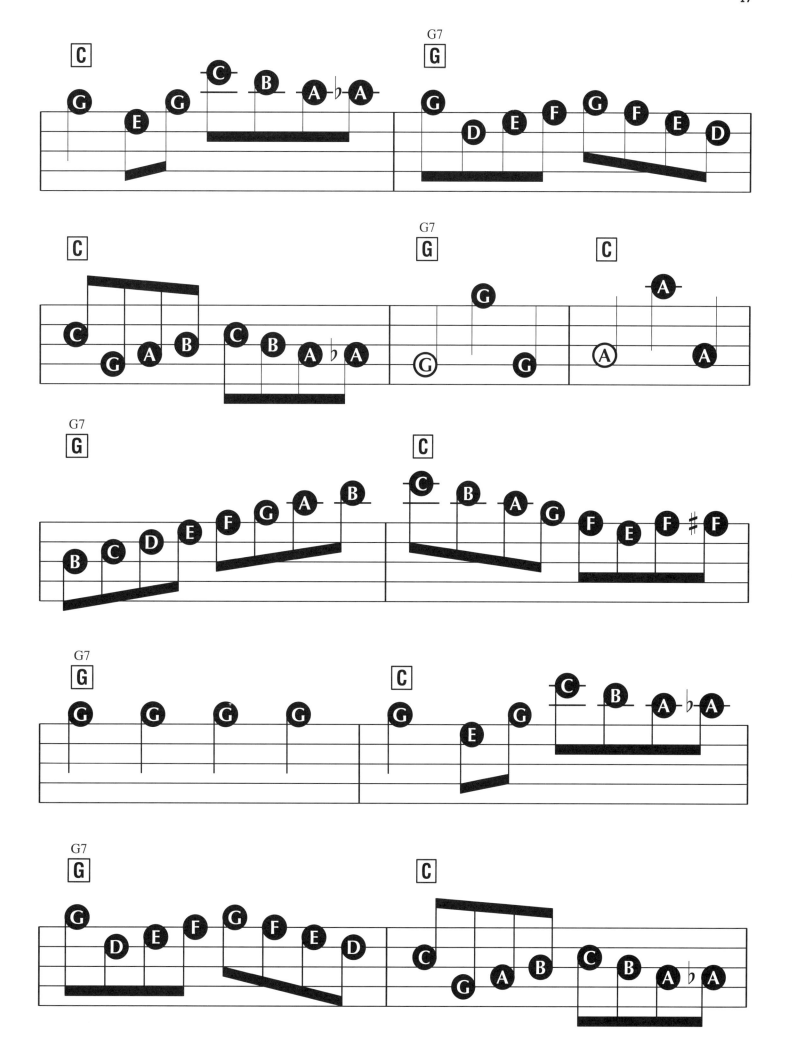

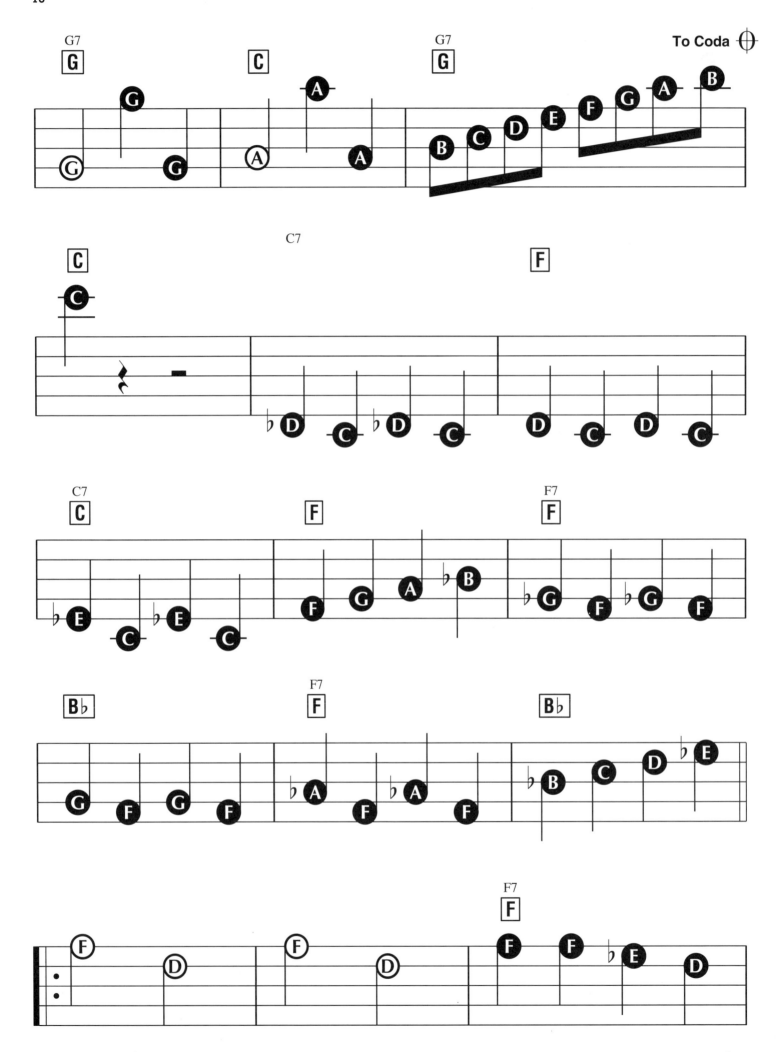

19

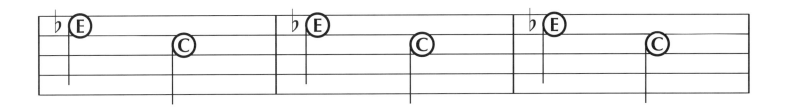

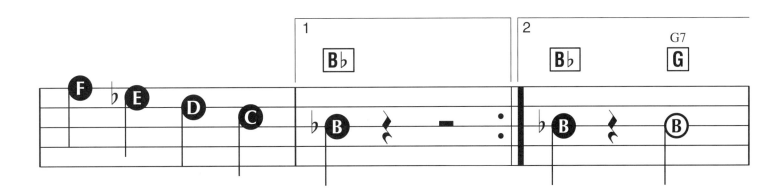

D.S. al Coda
(Return to 𝄋
Play to ⊕ and
Skip to Coda)

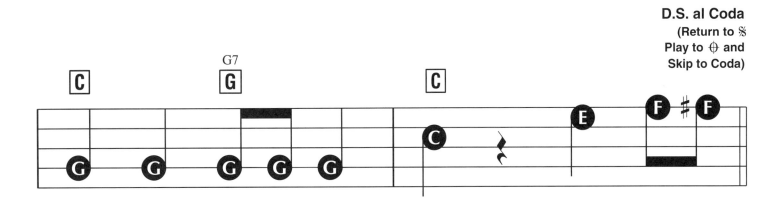

CODA
⊕

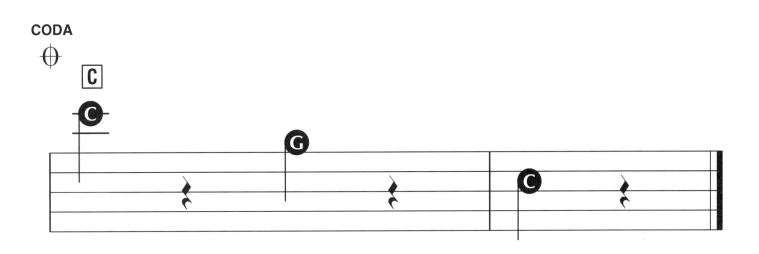

C-H-R-I-S-T-M-A-S

Registration 5
Rhythm: Fox Trot or Ballad

Words by Jenny Lou Carson
Music by Eddy Arnold

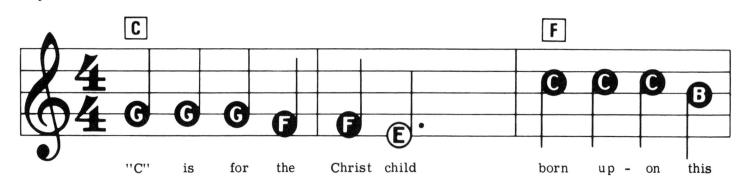
"C" is for the Christ child born up-on this

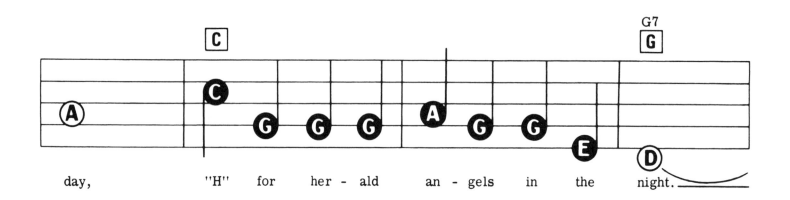
day, "H" for her-ald an-gels in the night.

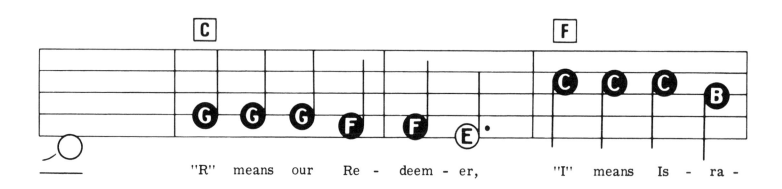
"R" means our Re-deem-er, "I" means Is-ra-

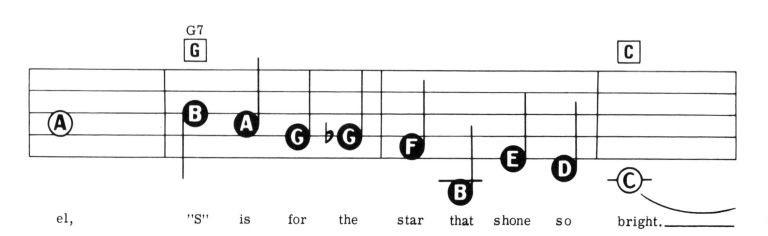
el, "S" is for the star that shone so bright.

Copyright © 1949 by Hill & Range Songs, Inc.
Copyright Renewed
All Rights Administered by Unichappell Music Inc.
International Copyright Secured   All Rights Reserved

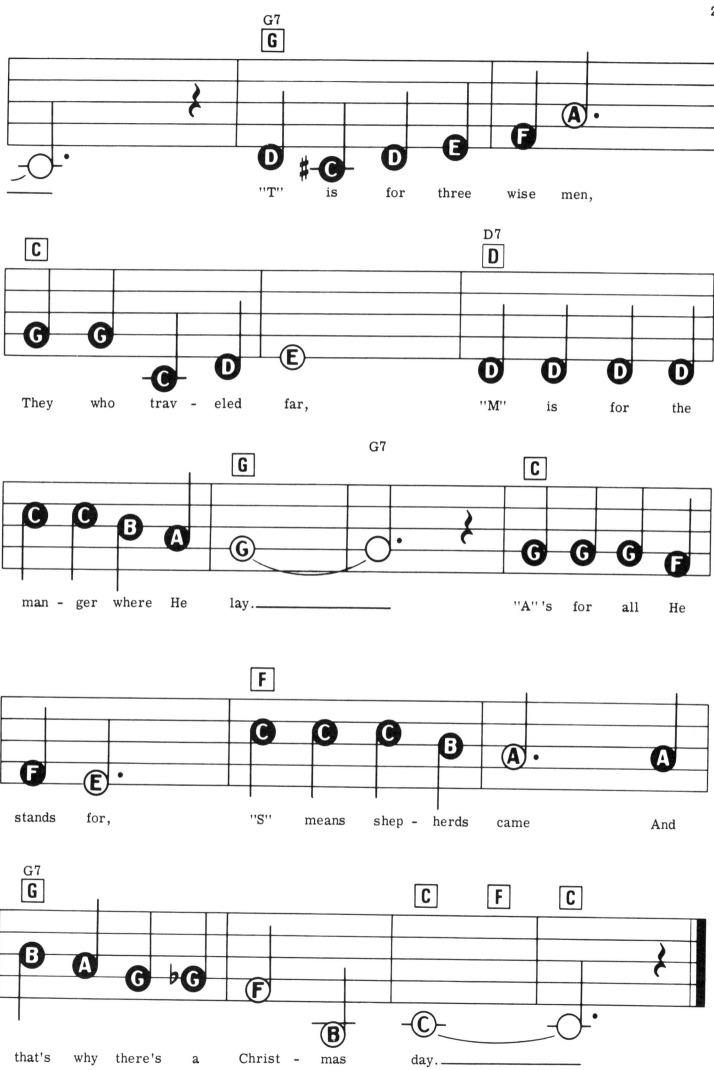

Christmas Is

Registration 10
Rhythm: Fox Trot or Slow Swing

Lyrics by Spence Maxwell
Music by Percy Faith

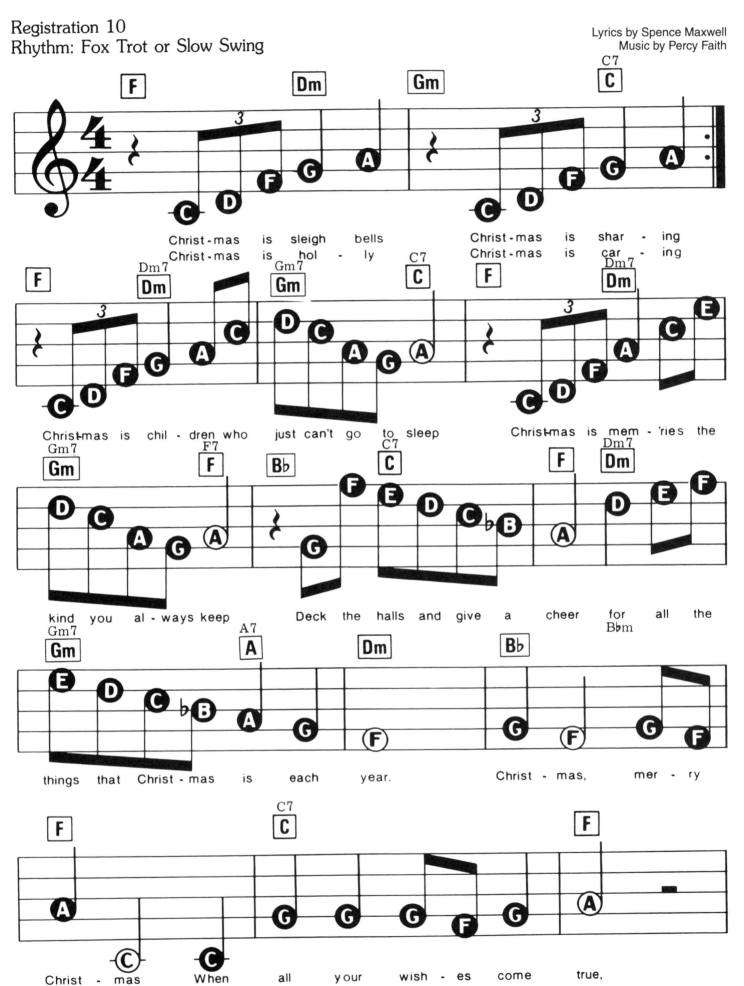

Copyright © 1966 UNIVERSAL - POLYGRAM INTERNATIONAL PUBLISHING, INC.
Copyright Renewed
All Rights Reserved   Used by Permission

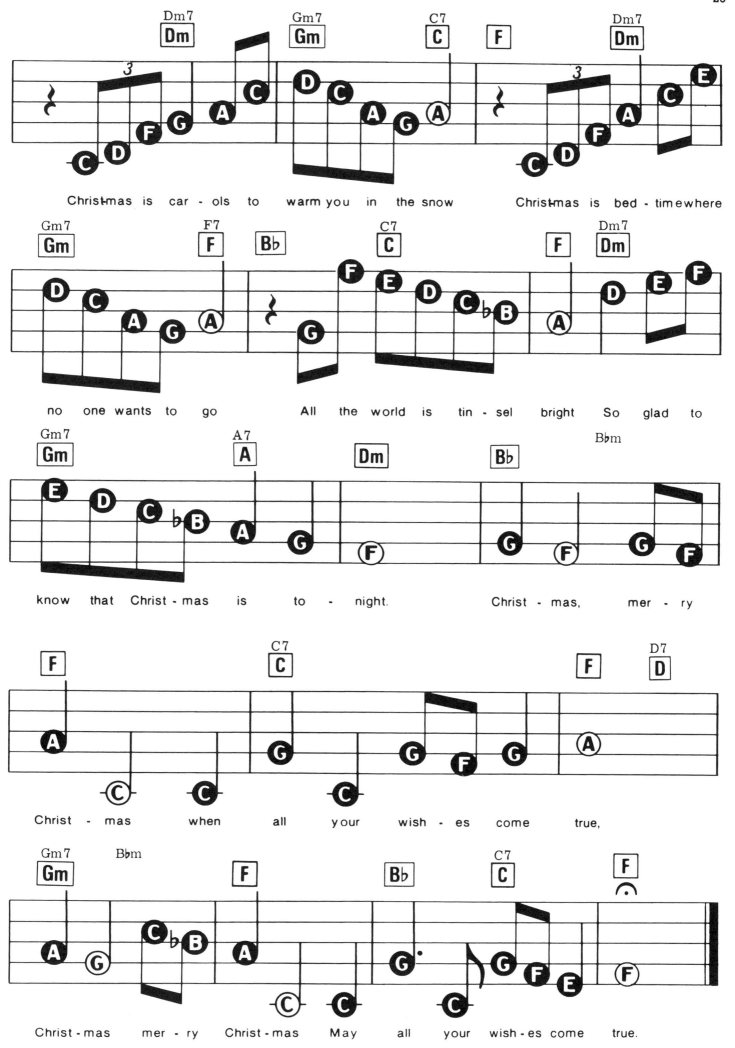

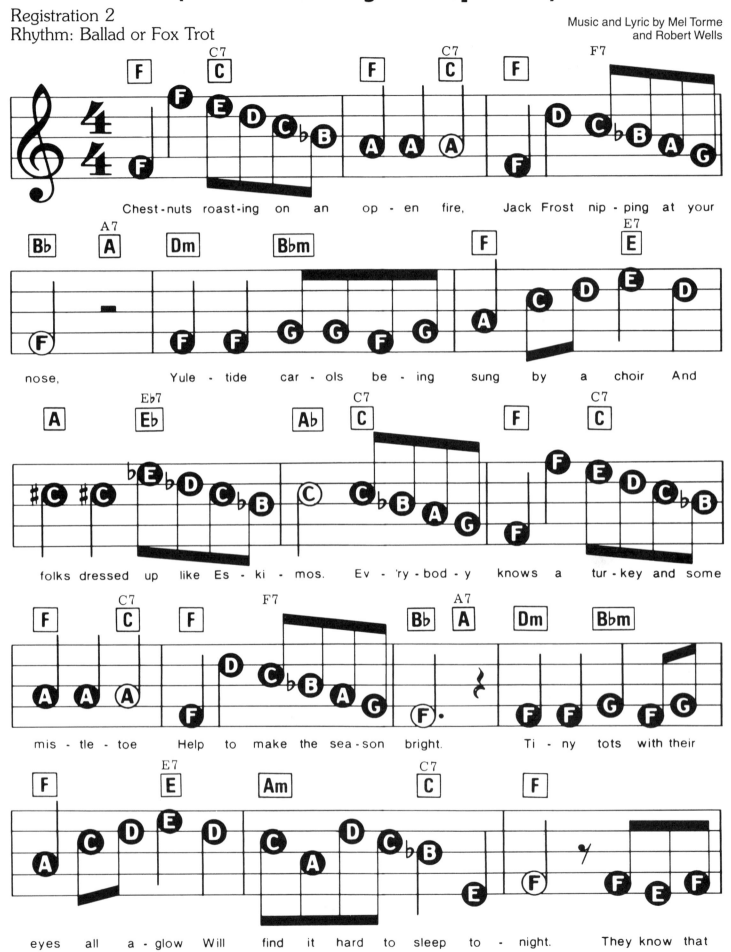

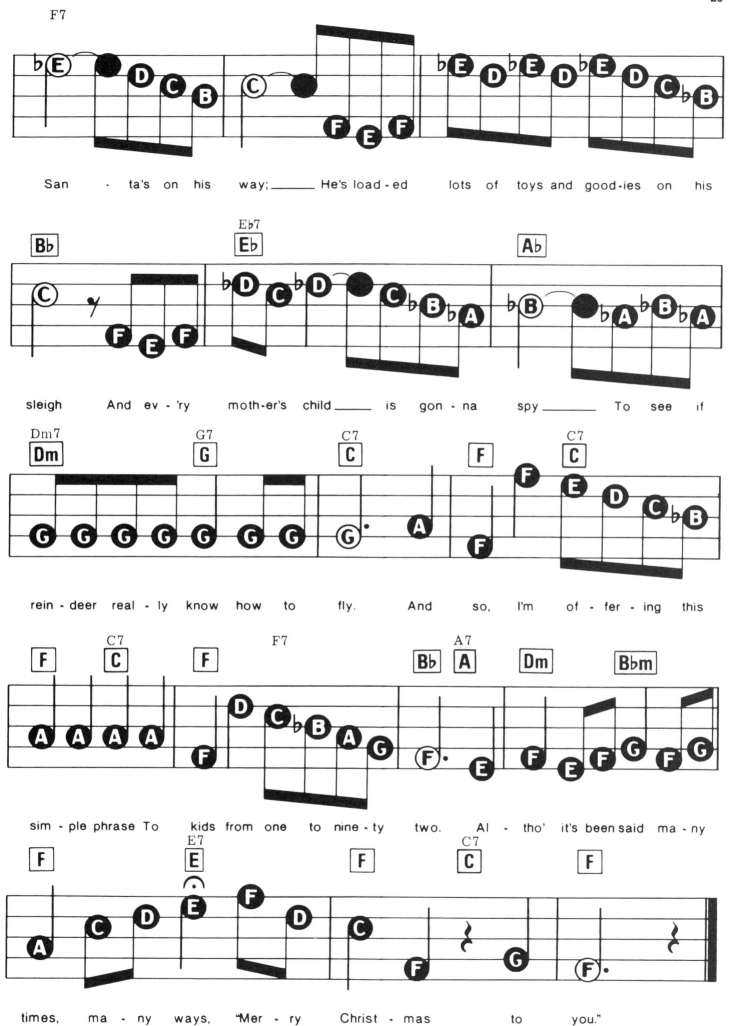

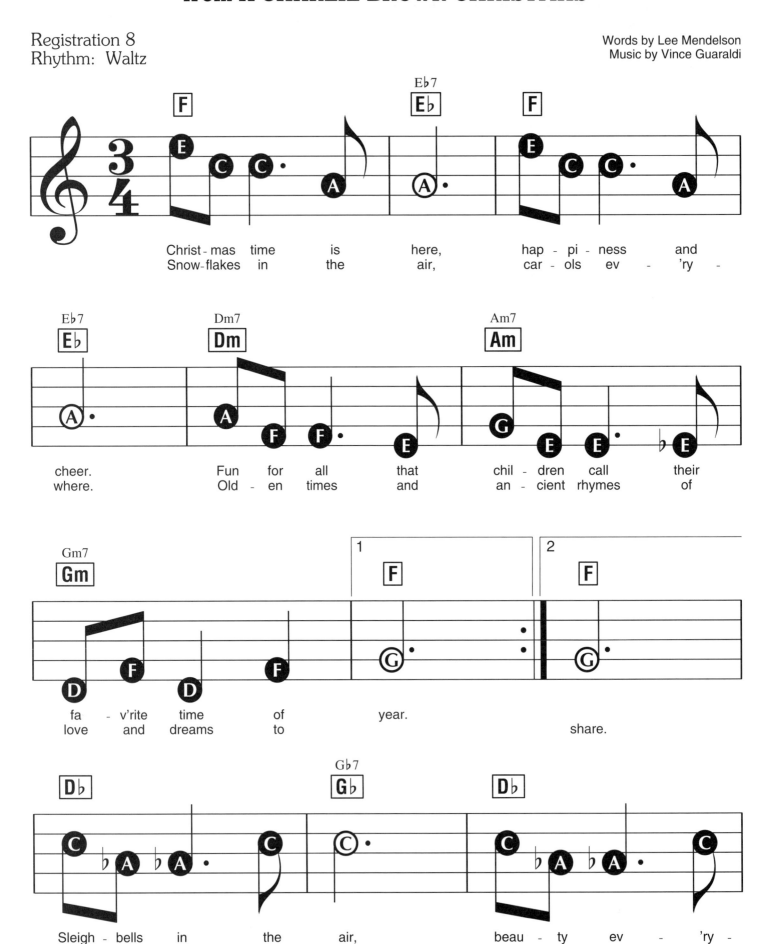

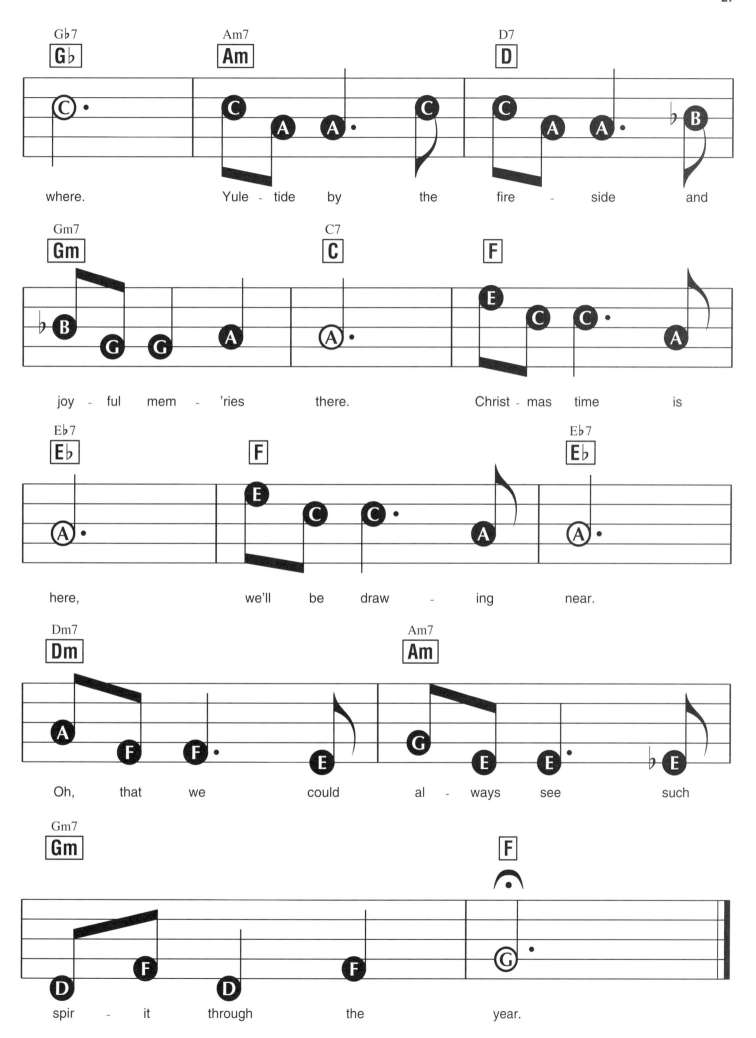

Feliz Navidad

Registration 1
Rhythm: Latin or Bossa Nova

Music and Lyrics by
José Feliciano

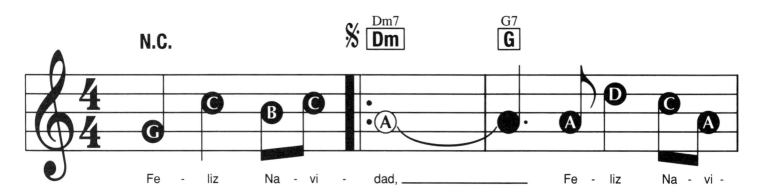

Fe - liz Na - vi - dad, _____ Fe - liz Na - vi -

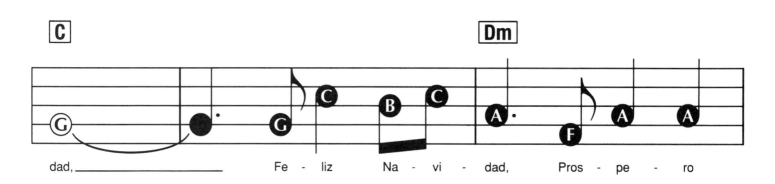

dad, _____ Fe - liz Na - vi - dad, Pros - pe - ro

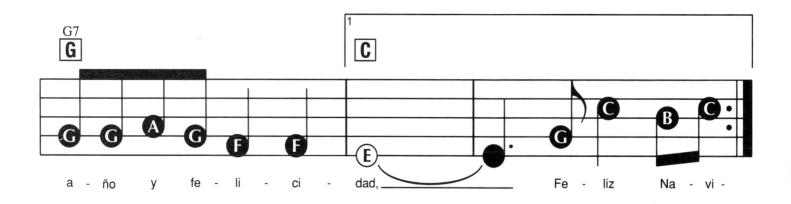

a - ño y fe - li - ci - dad, _____ Fe - liz Na - vi -

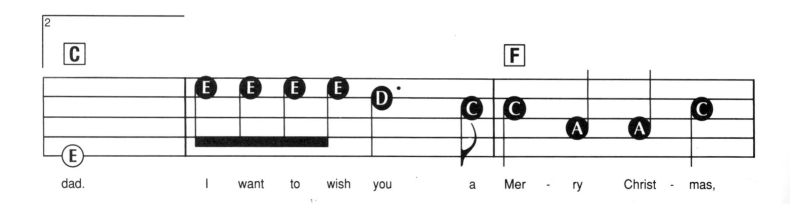

dad. I want to wish you a Mer - ry Christ - mas,

Copyright © 1970 J & H Publishing Company (ASCAP)
Copyright Renewed
All Rights Administered by Stollman and Stollman o/b/o J & H Publishing Company
International Copyright Secured All Rights Reserved

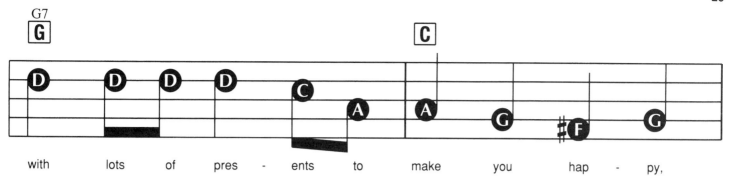
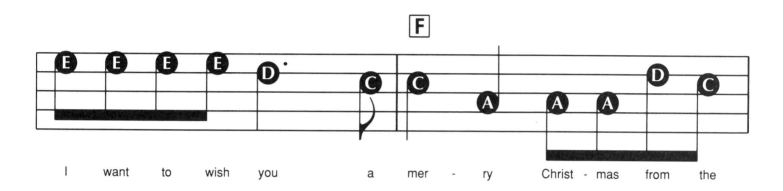
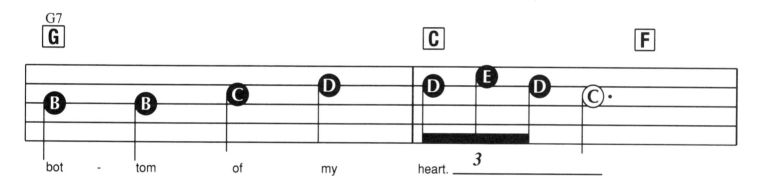
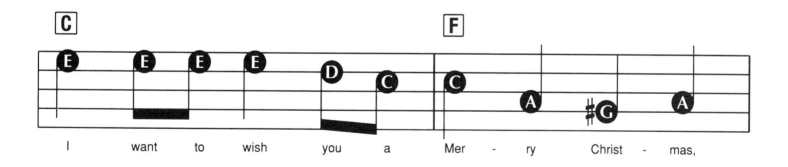
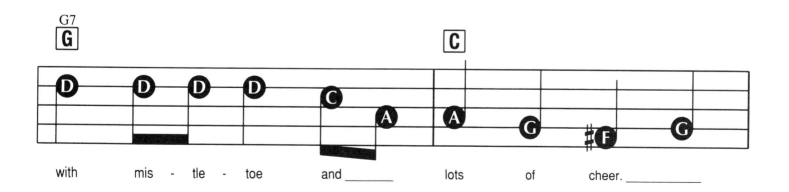

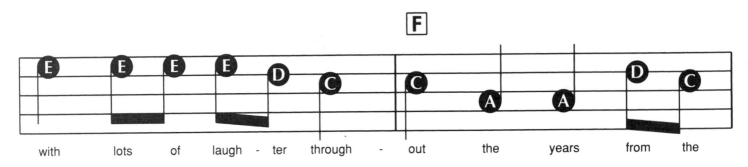
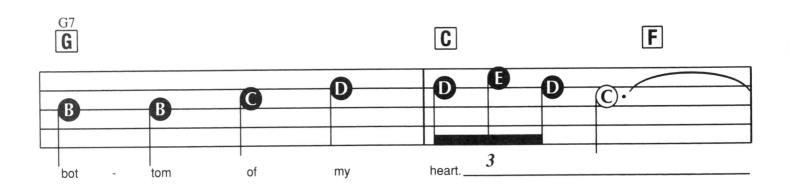
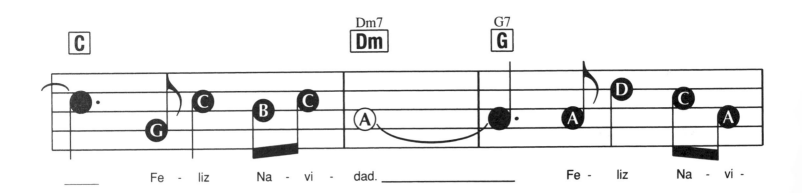
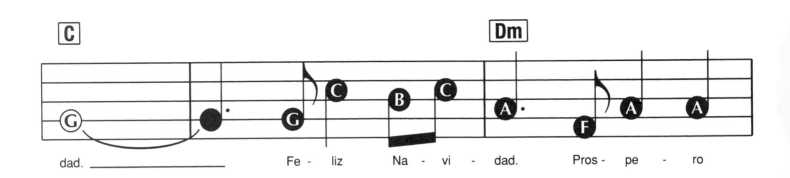
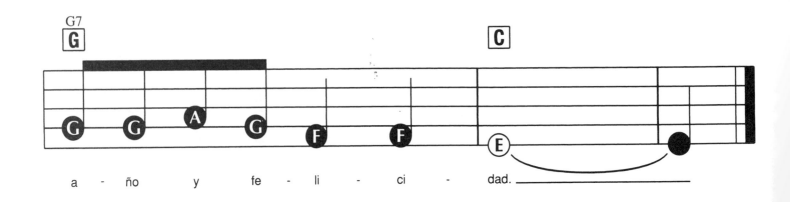

Frosty the Snow Man

Registration 2
Rhythm: Fox Trot or Swing

Words and Music by Steve Nelson
and Jack Rollins

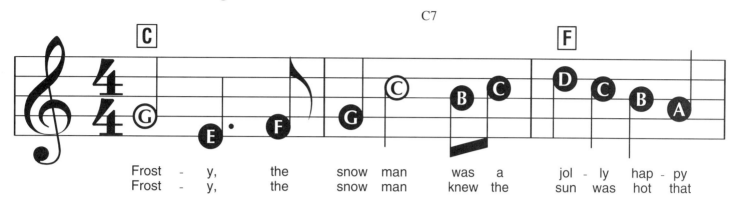

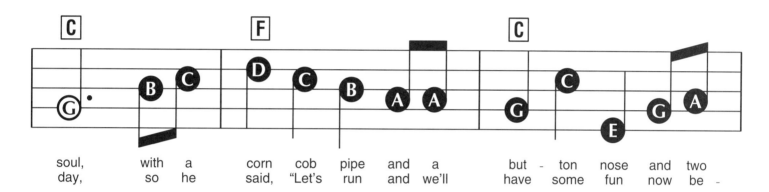

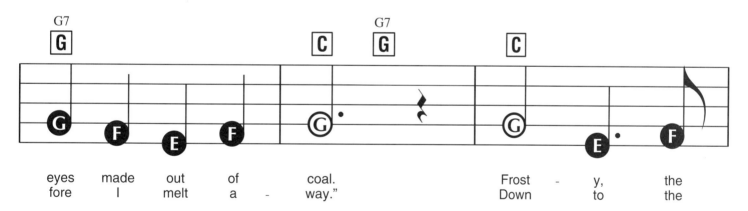

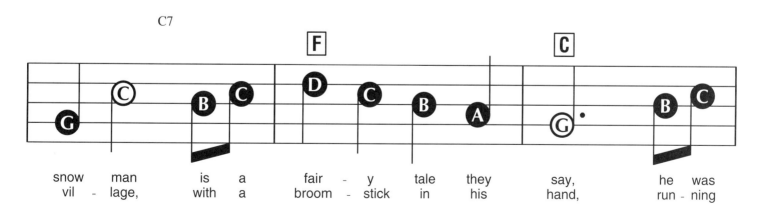

Copyright © 1950 by Chappell & Co.
Copyright Renewed
International Copyright Secured   All Rights Reserved

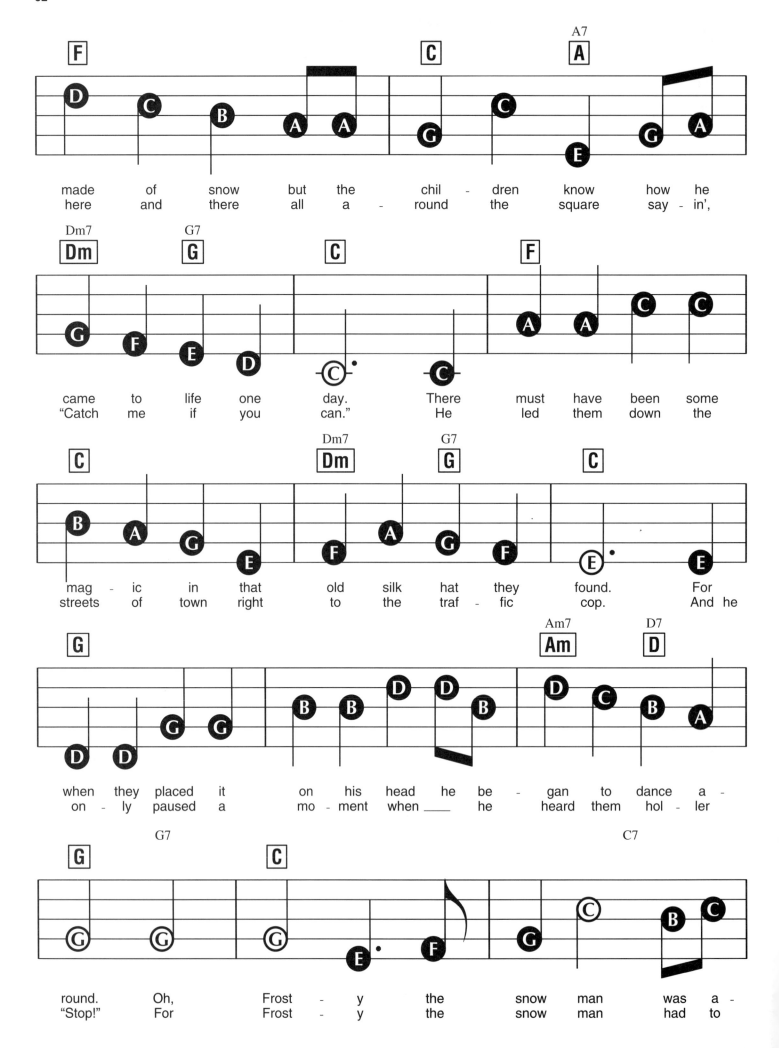

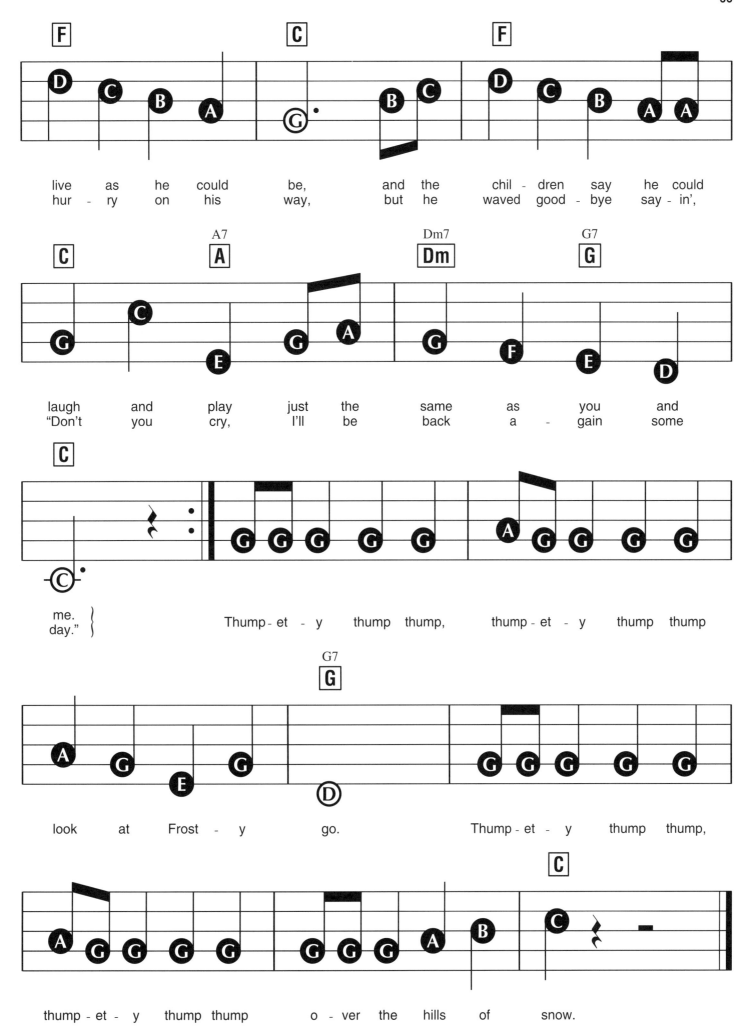

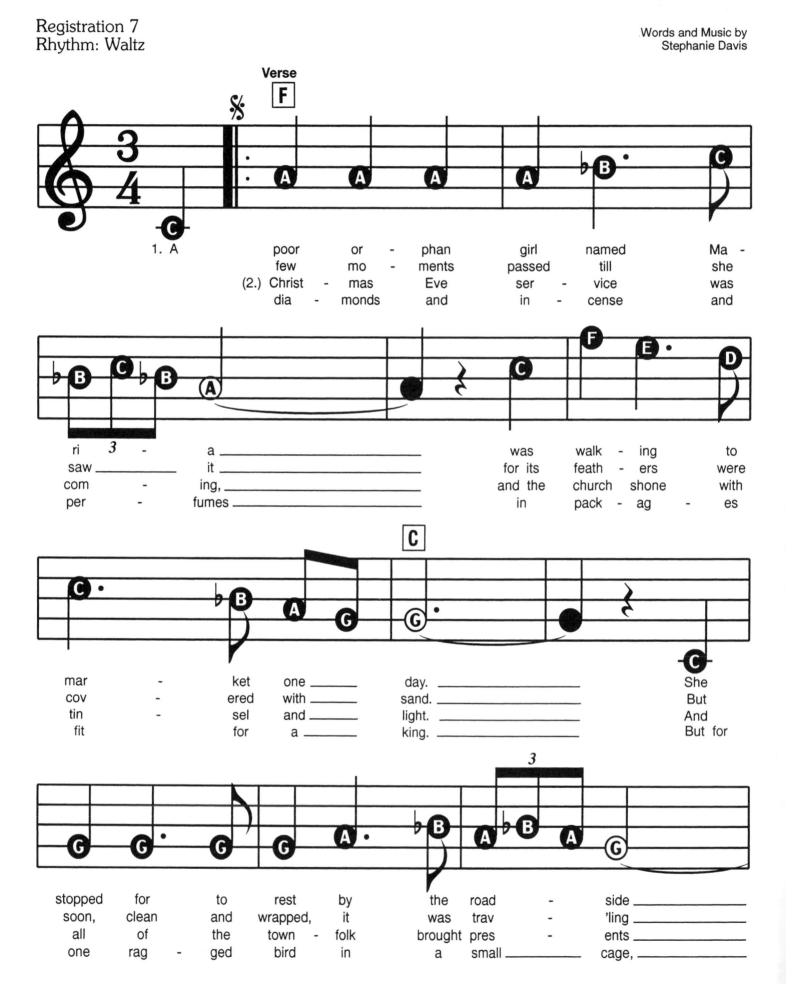

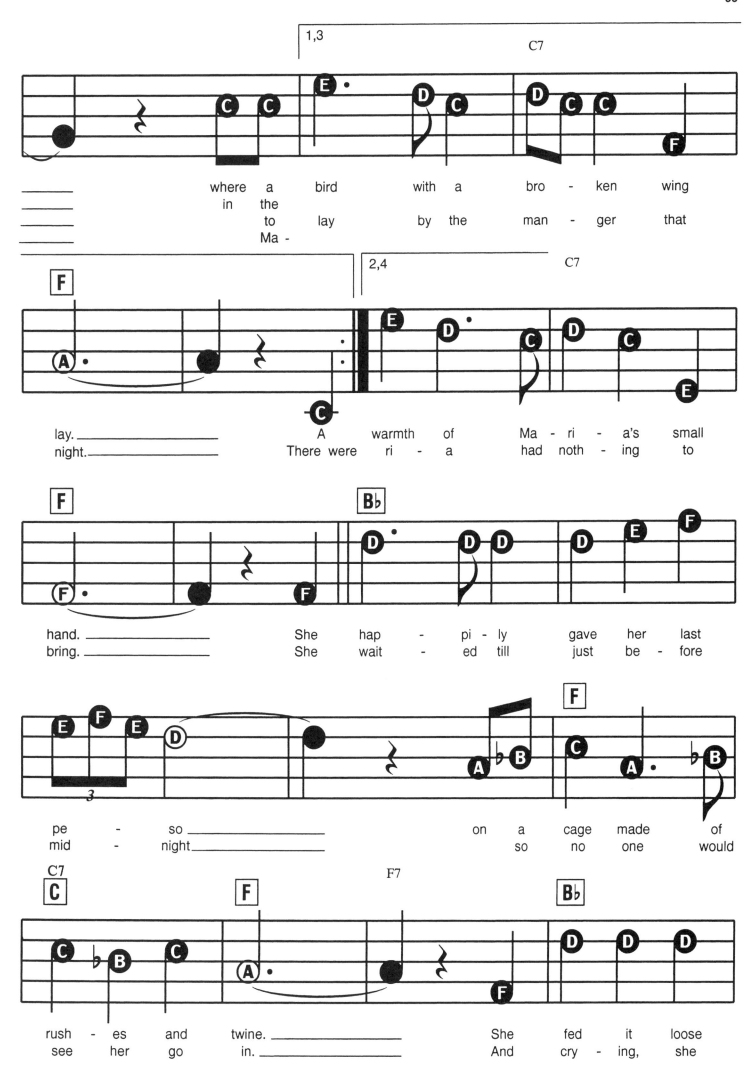

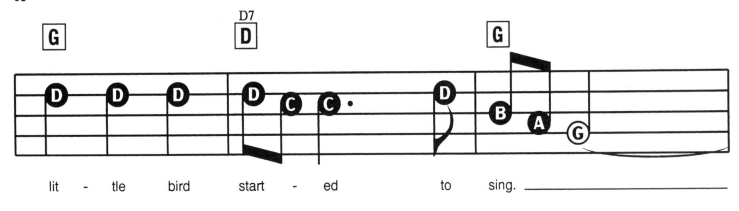
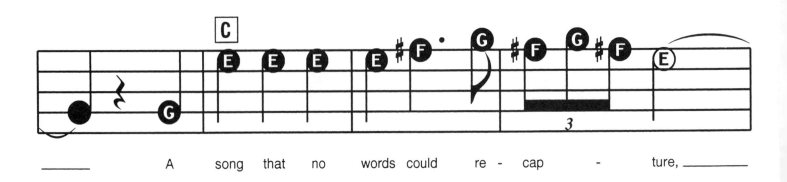
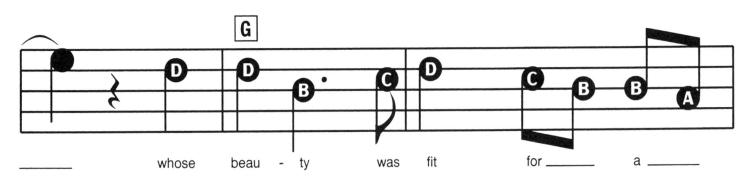
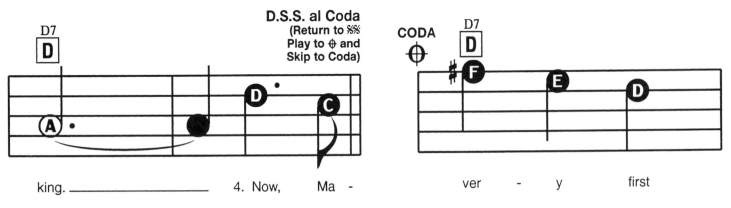
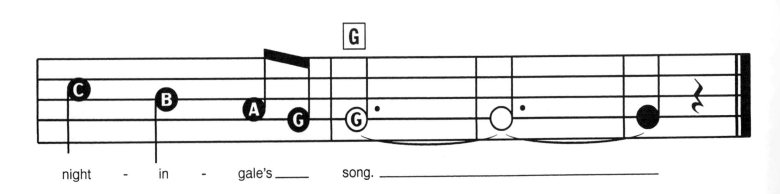

Grandma Got Run Over by a Reindeer

Registration 2
Rhythm: Fox Trot or Swing

Words and Music by
Randy Brooks

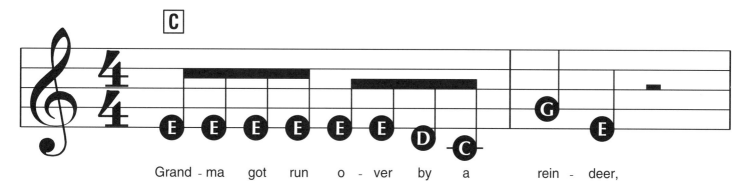
Grand-ma got run o-ver by a rein-deer,

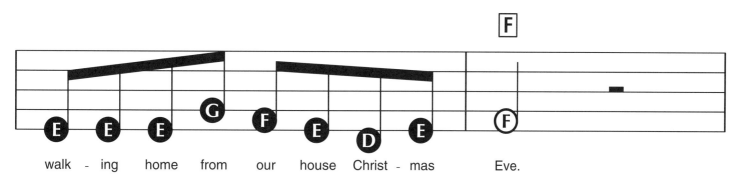
walk-ing home from our house Christ-mas Eve.

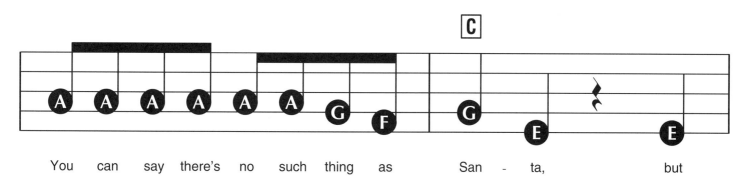
You can say there's no such thing as San-ta, but

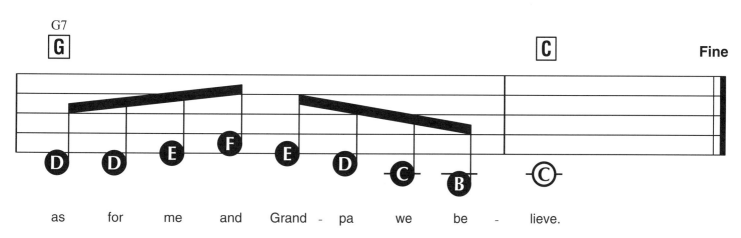
as for me and Grand-pa we be-lieve.

Copyright © 1984 by Kris Publishing (SESAC) and Elmo Publishing (SESAC)
Admin. by ICG
All Rights Reserved   Used by Permission

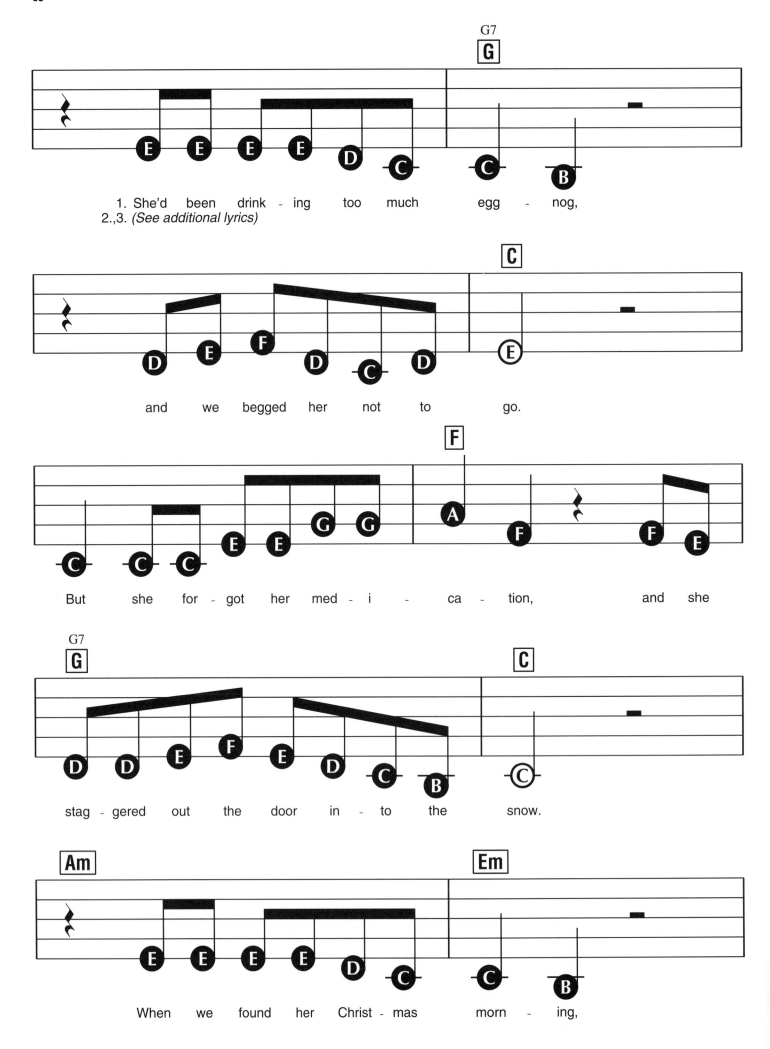

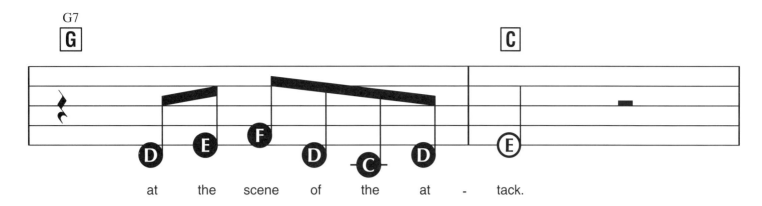
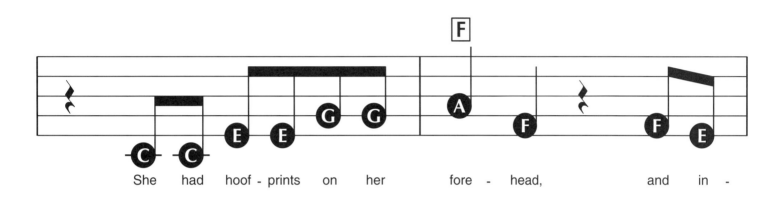
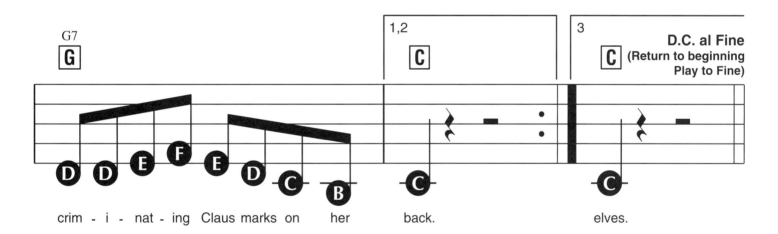

Additional Lyrics

2. Now we're all so proud of Grandpa,
   he's been taking this so well.
   See him in there watching football,
   drinking beer and playing cards with Cousin Mel.
   It's not Christmas without Grandma,
   all the family's dressed in black,
   And we just can't help but wonder:
   should we open up her gifts or send them back? *(To Chorus:)*

3. Now the goose is on the table,
   and the pudding made of fig.
   And the blue and silver candles,
   That would just have matched the hair in Grandma's wig.
   I've warned all my friends and neighbors,
   better watch out for yourselves.
   They should never give a license,
   to a man who drives a sleigh and plays with elves. *(To Chorus:)*

Grown-Up Christmas List

Registration 1
Rhythm: 4/4 Ballad

Words and Music by David Foster and Linda Thompson-Jenner

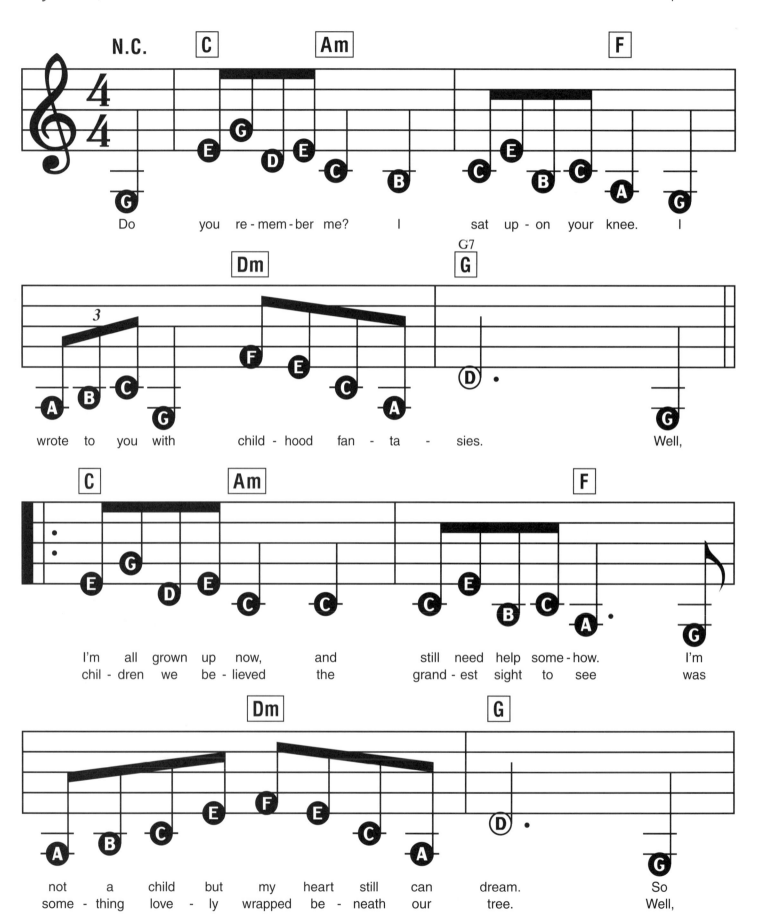

Copyright © 1990 by Air Bear Music, Warner-Tamerlane Publishing Corp. and Linda's Boys Music
All Rights for Air Bear Music Administered by Peermusic Ltd.
All Rights for Linda's Boys Music Administered by Warner-Tamerlane Publishing Corp.
International Copyright Secured   All Rights Reserved

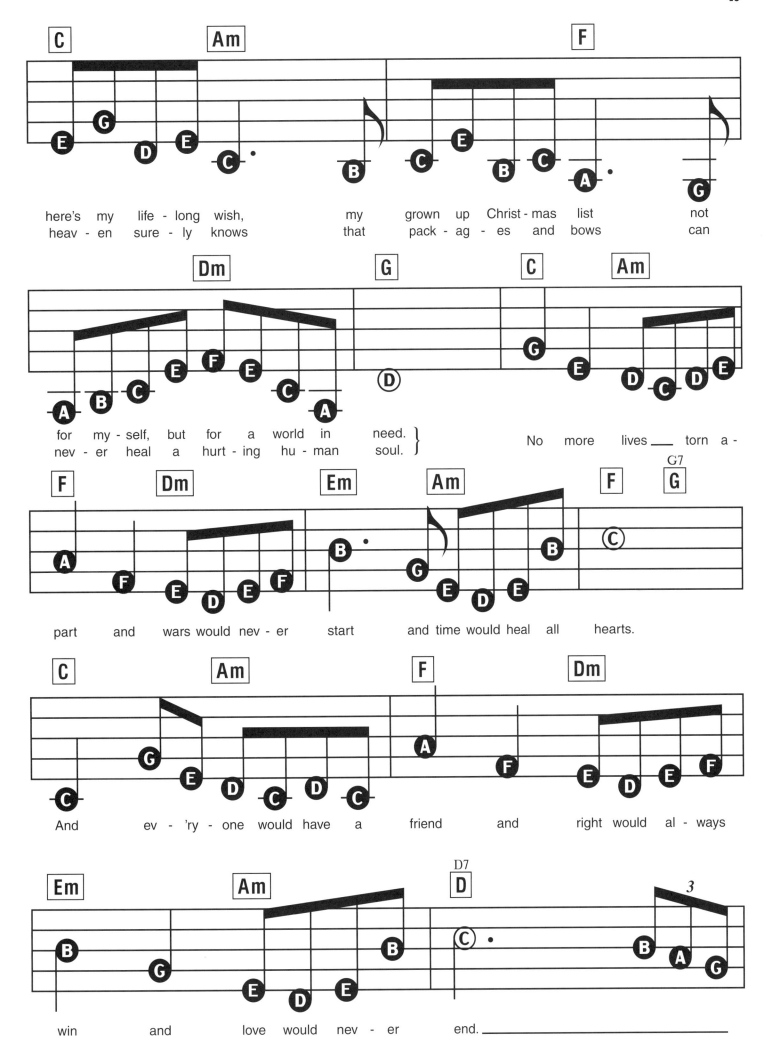

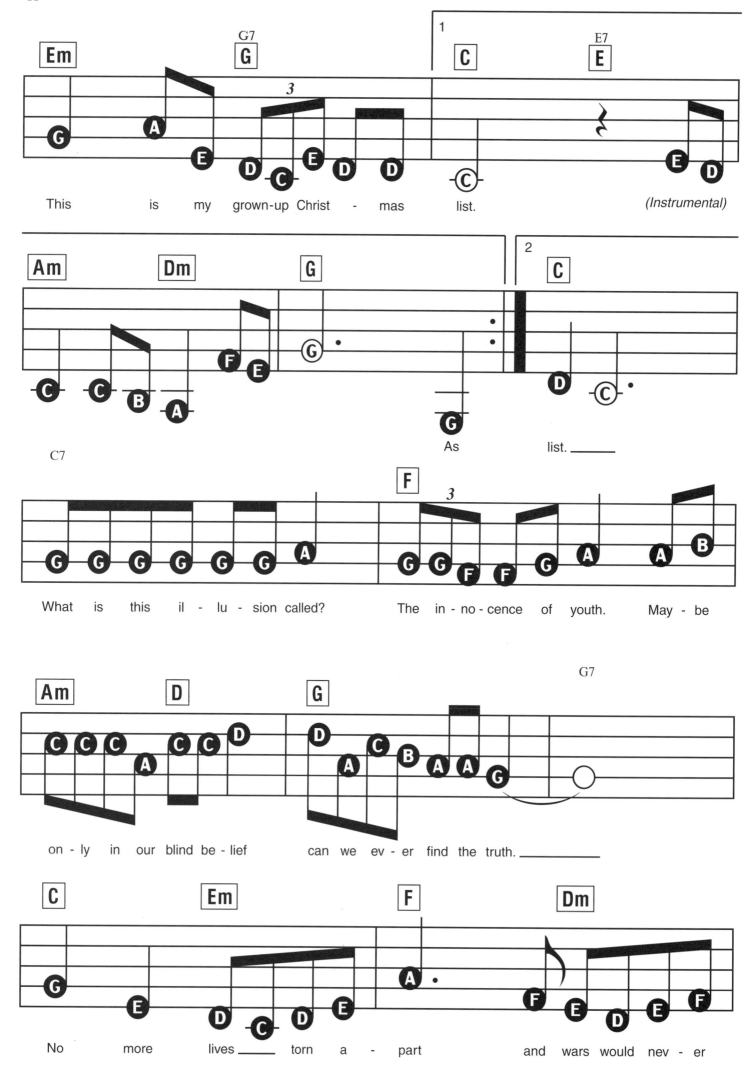

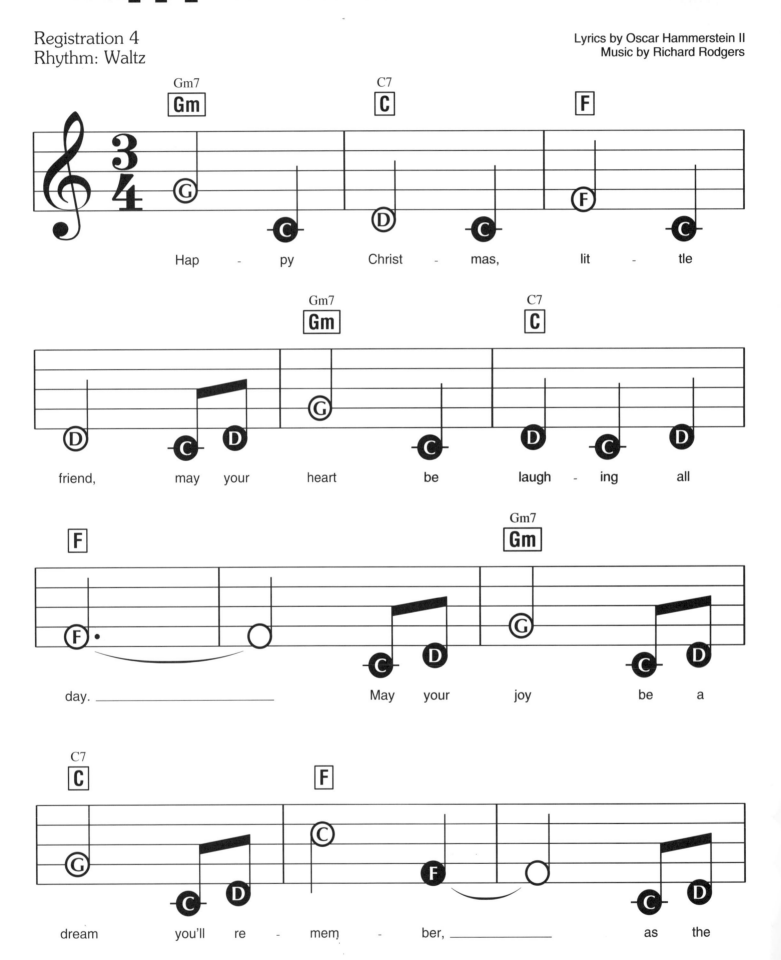

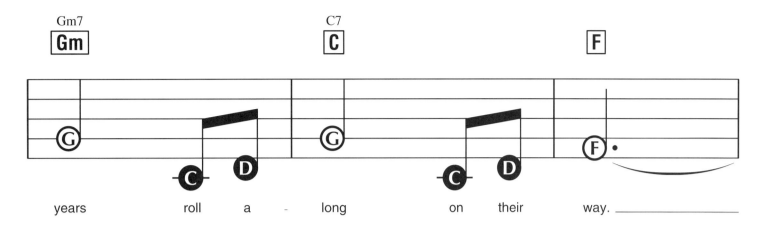
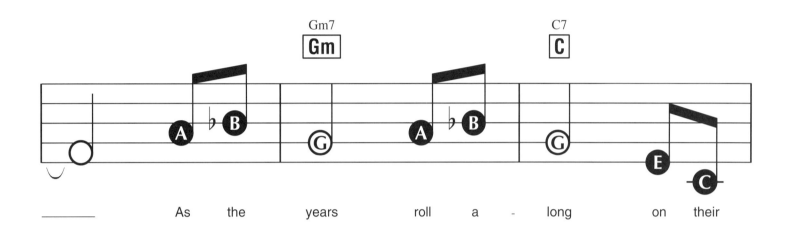
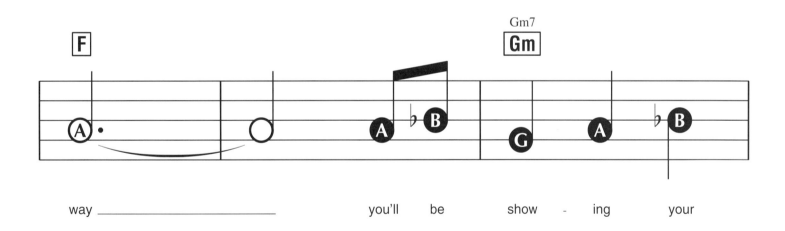
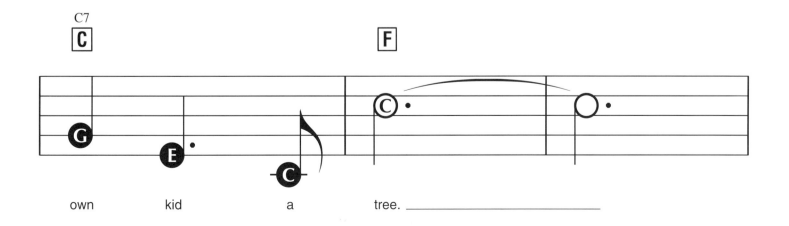

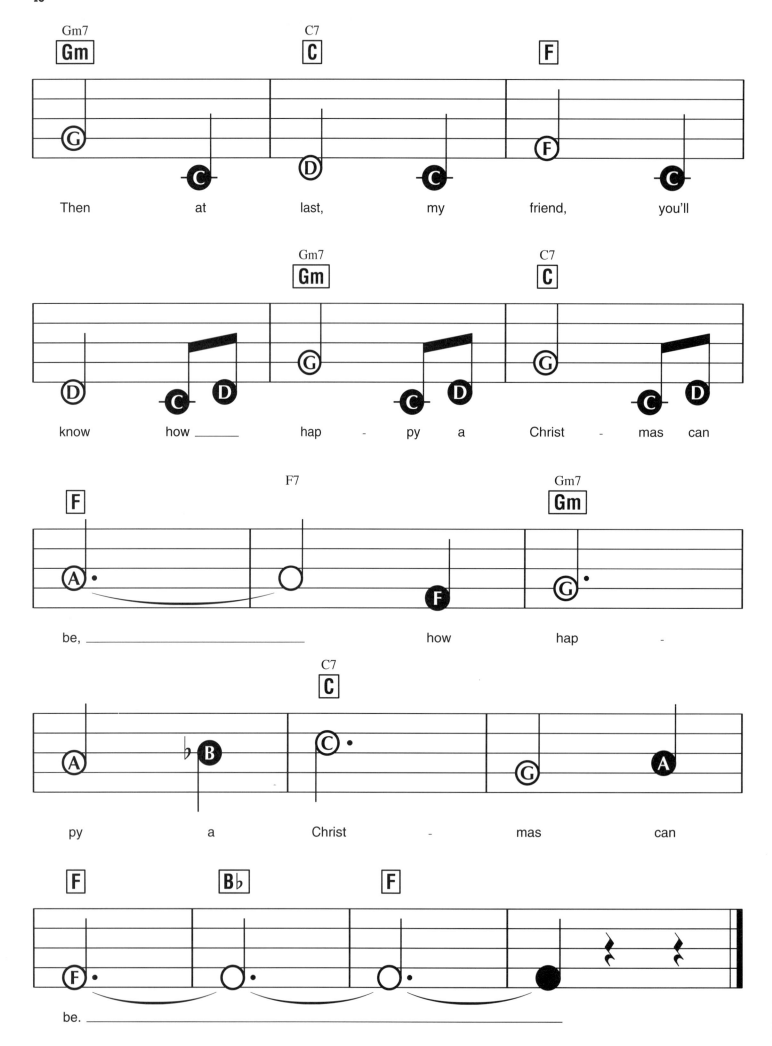

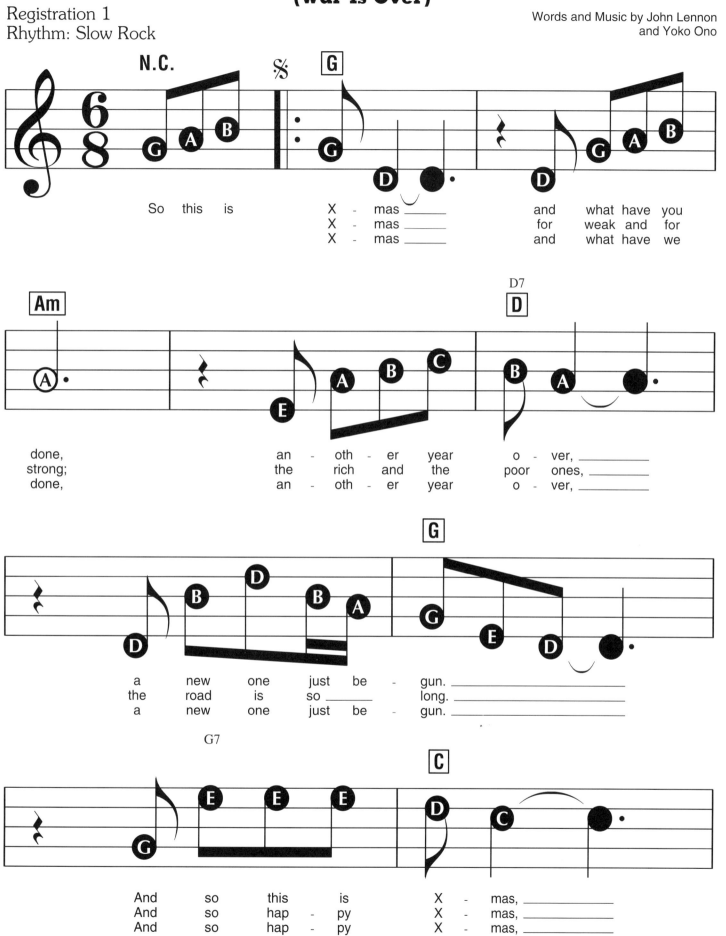

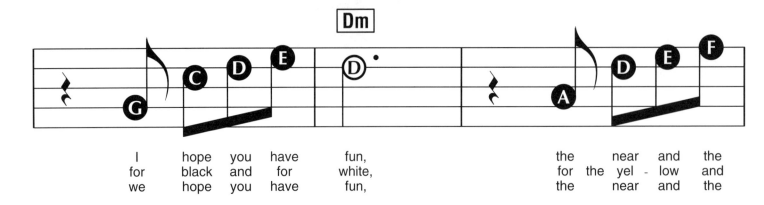
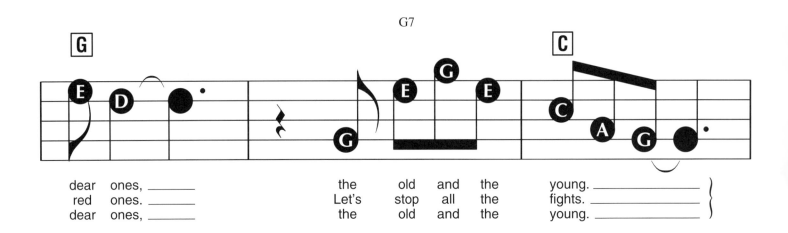
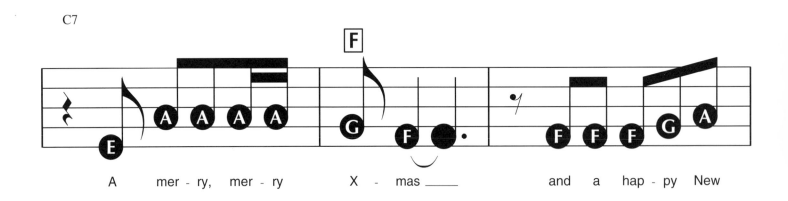
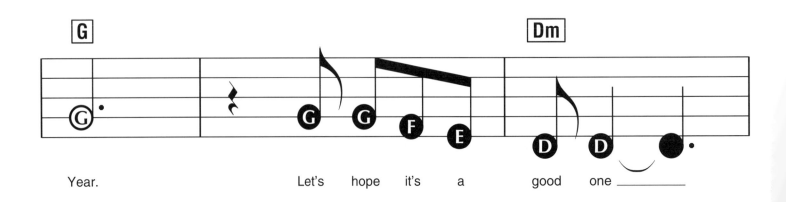

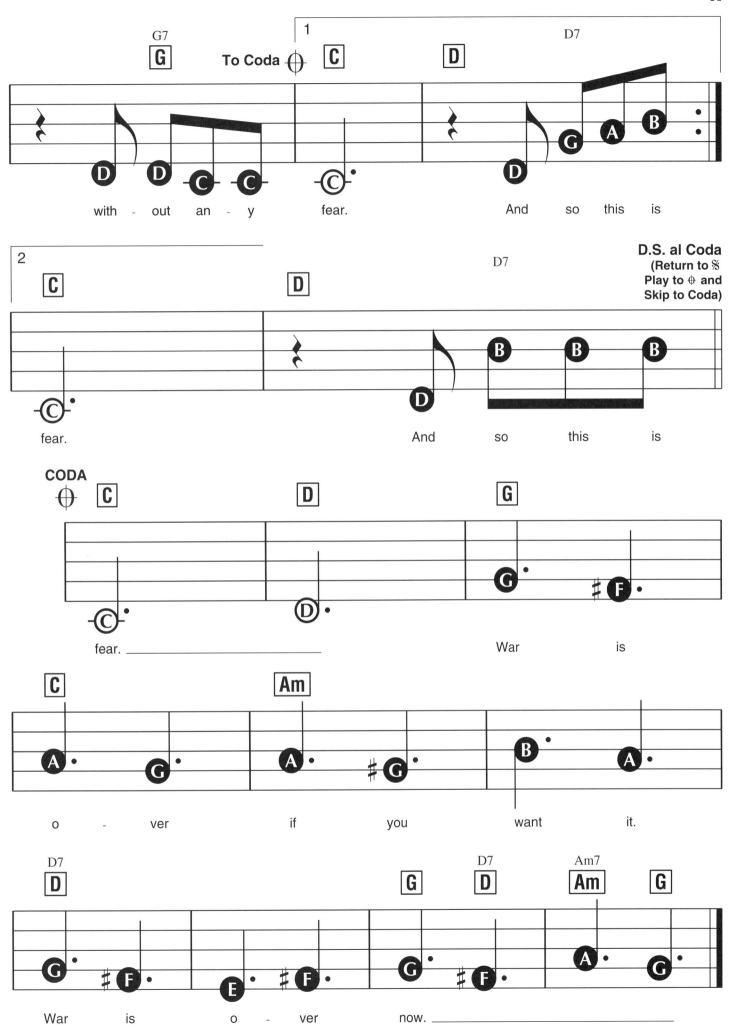

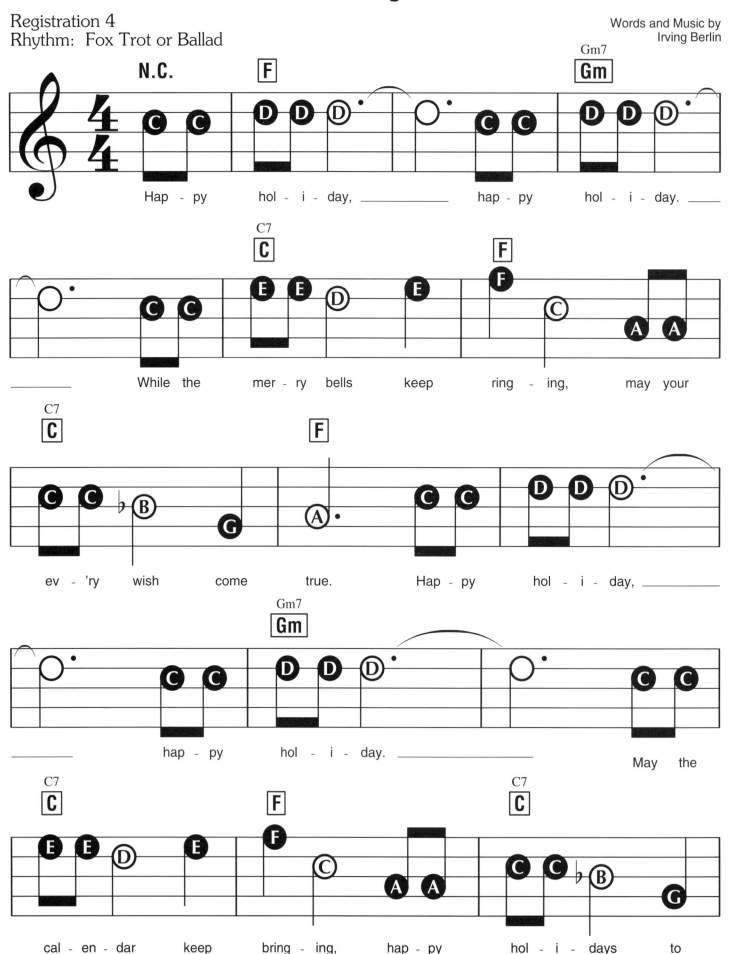

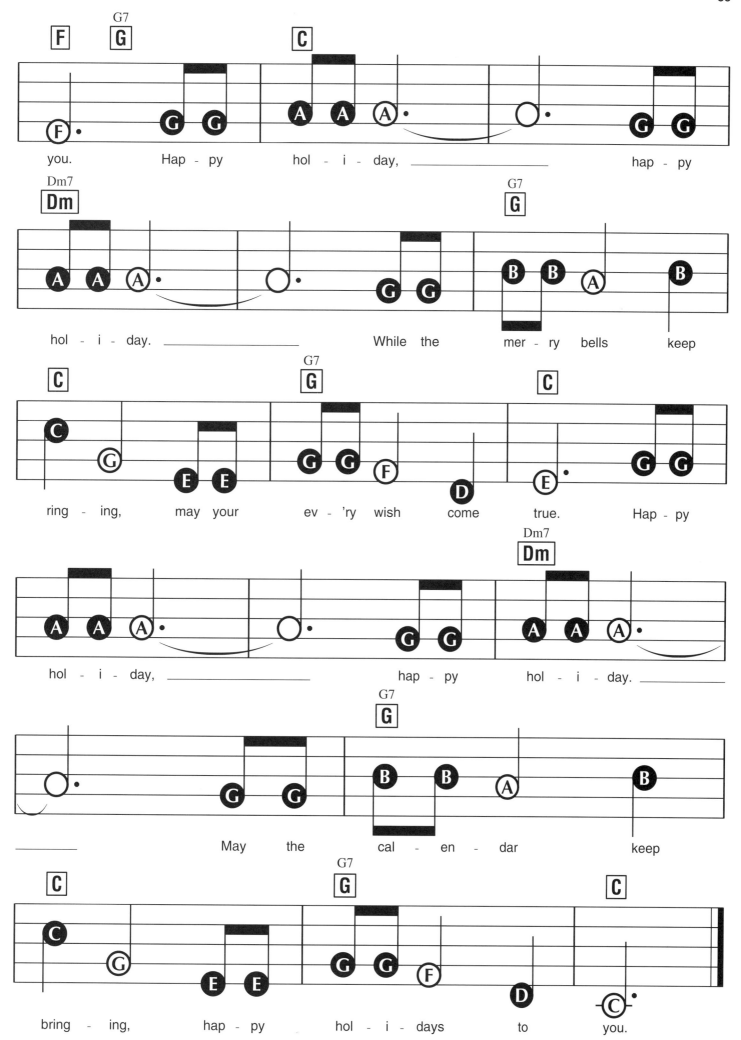

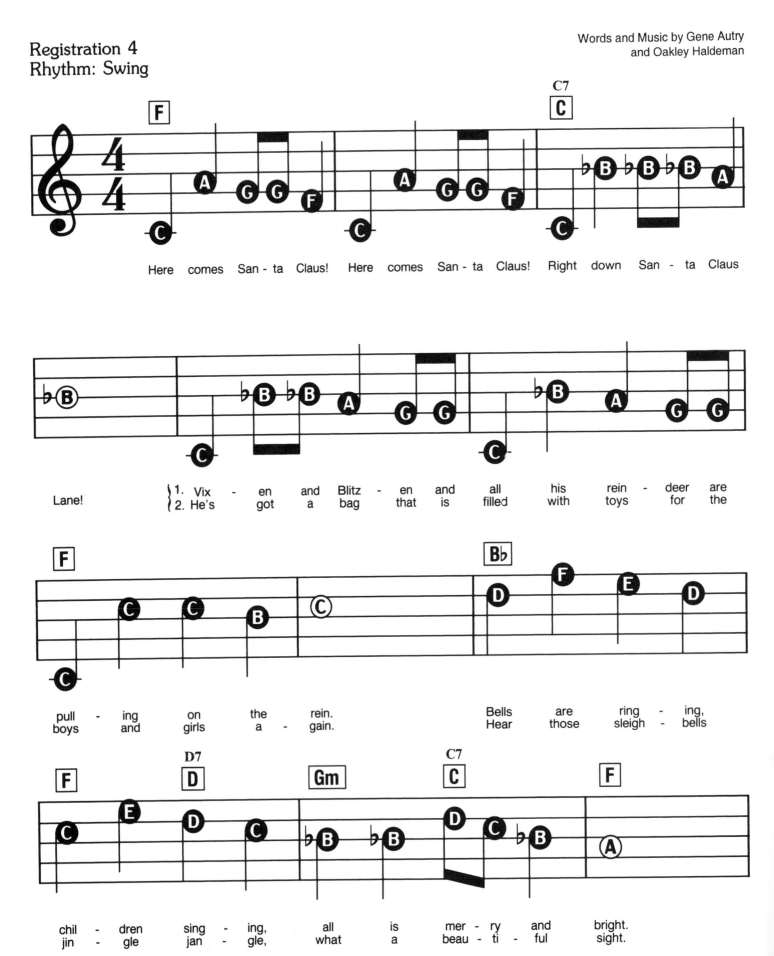

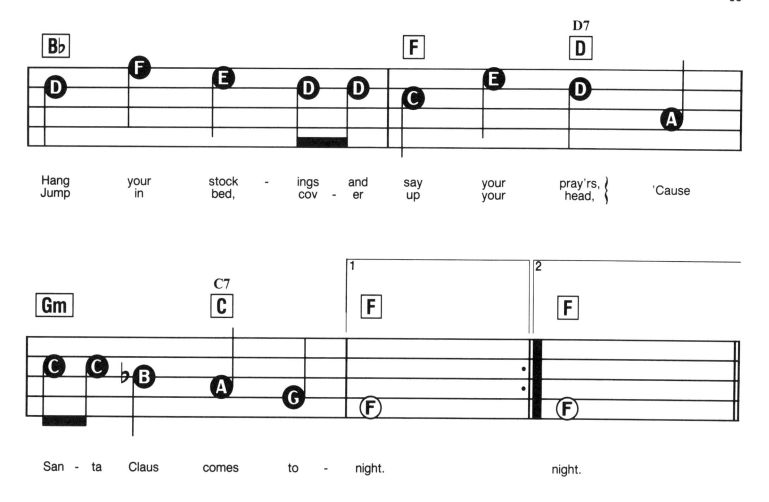
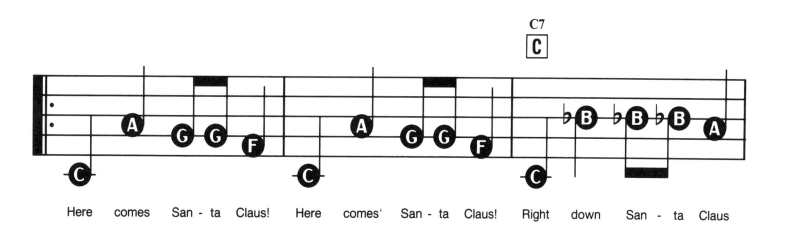
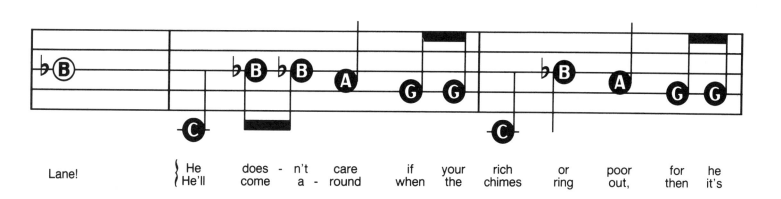

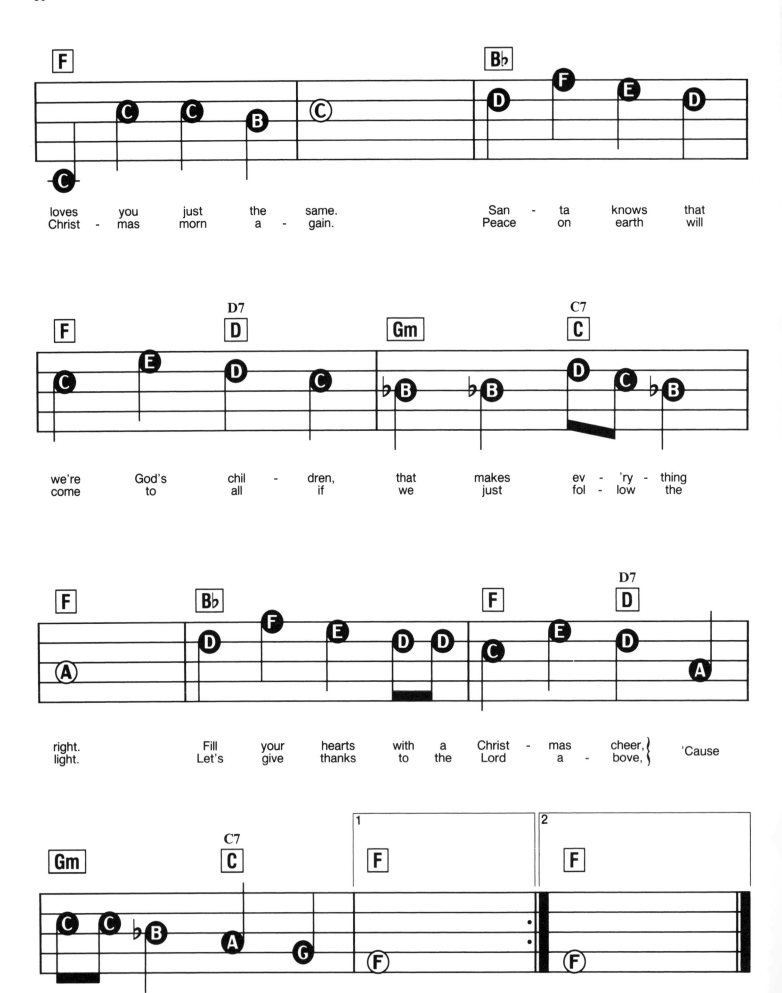

Hard Candy Christmas

Registration: 4
Rhythm: Country or Shuffle

Words and Music by
Carol Hall

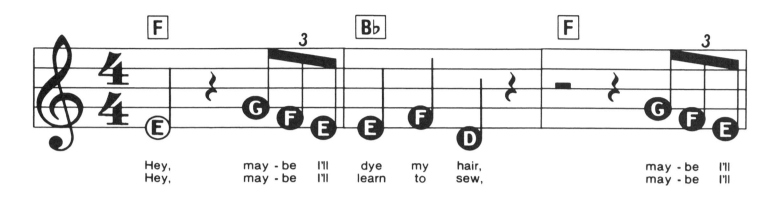
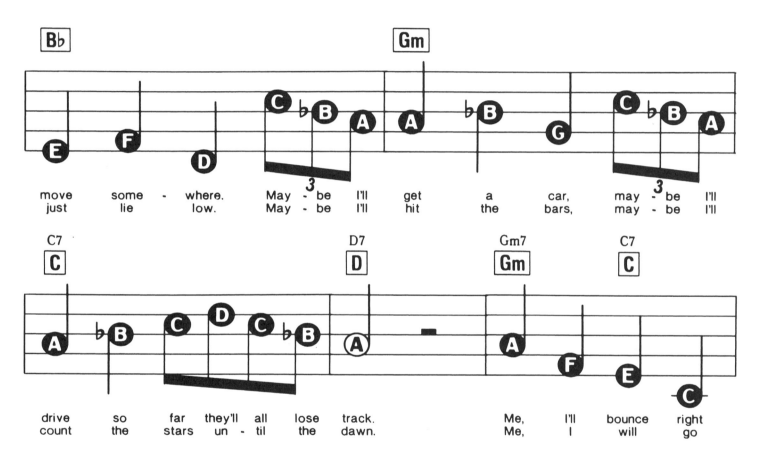
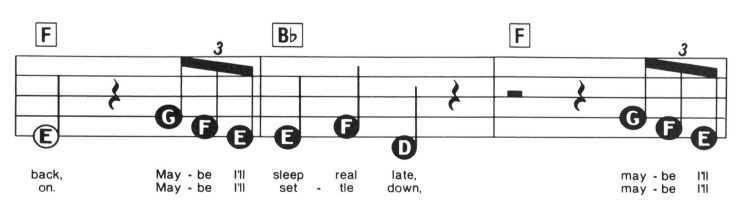

Copyright © 1978 DANIEL MUSIC LTD. and OTAY MUSIC CORP.
All Rights for the USA and Canada Controlled and Administered by UNIVERSAL MUSIC CORP.
All Rights Reserved Used by Permission

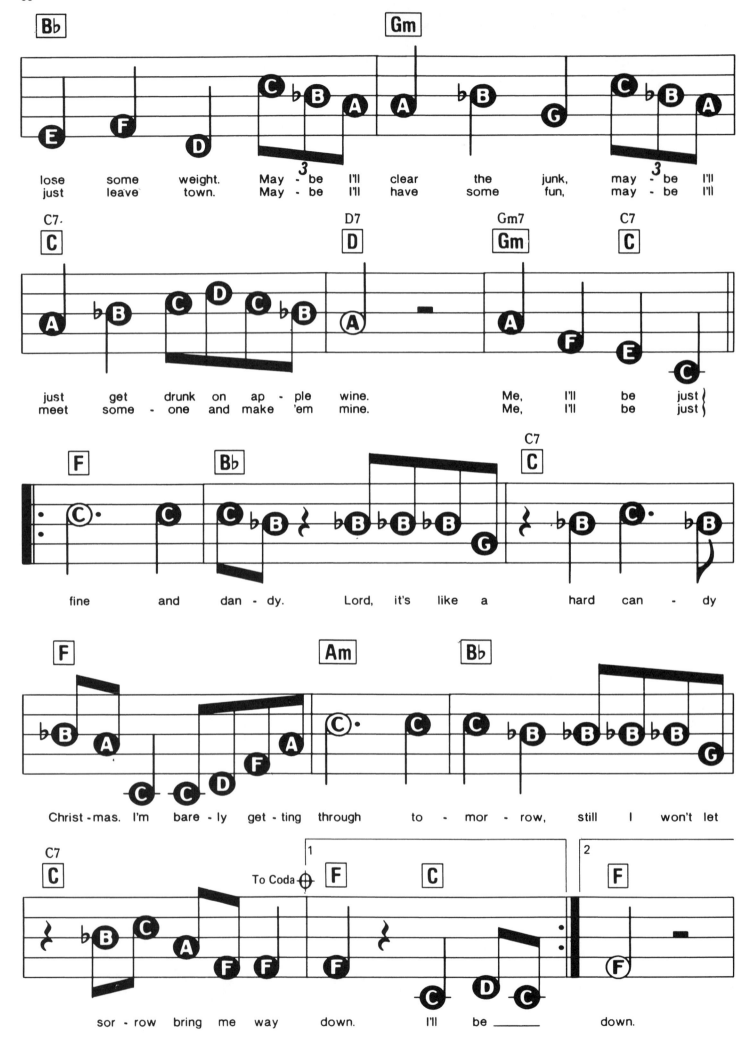

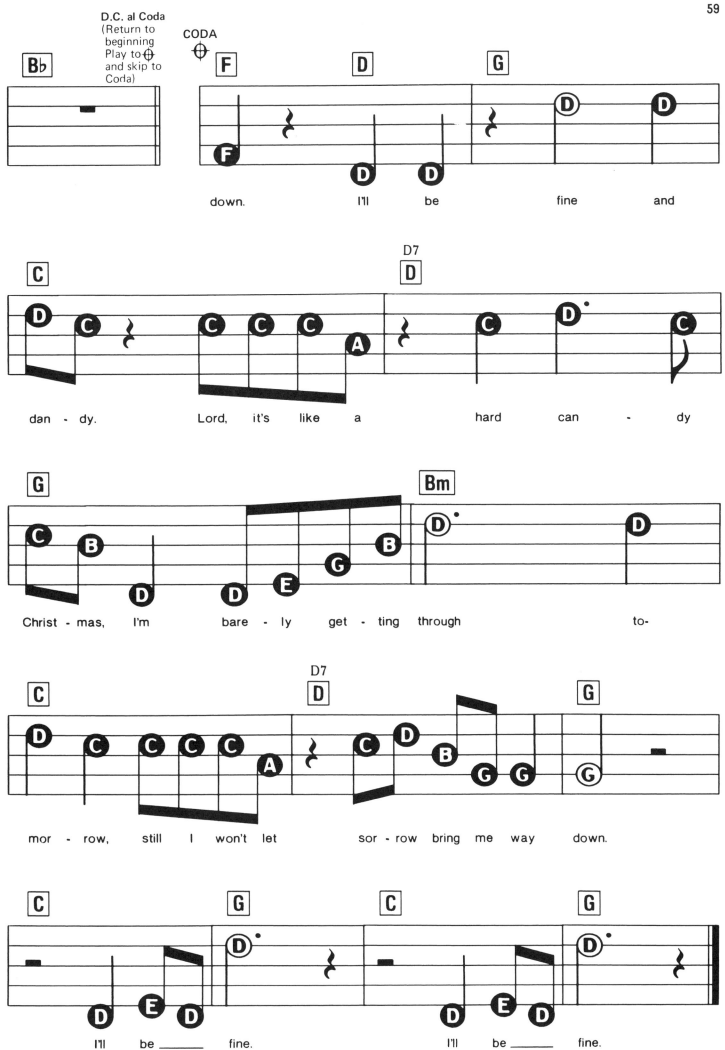

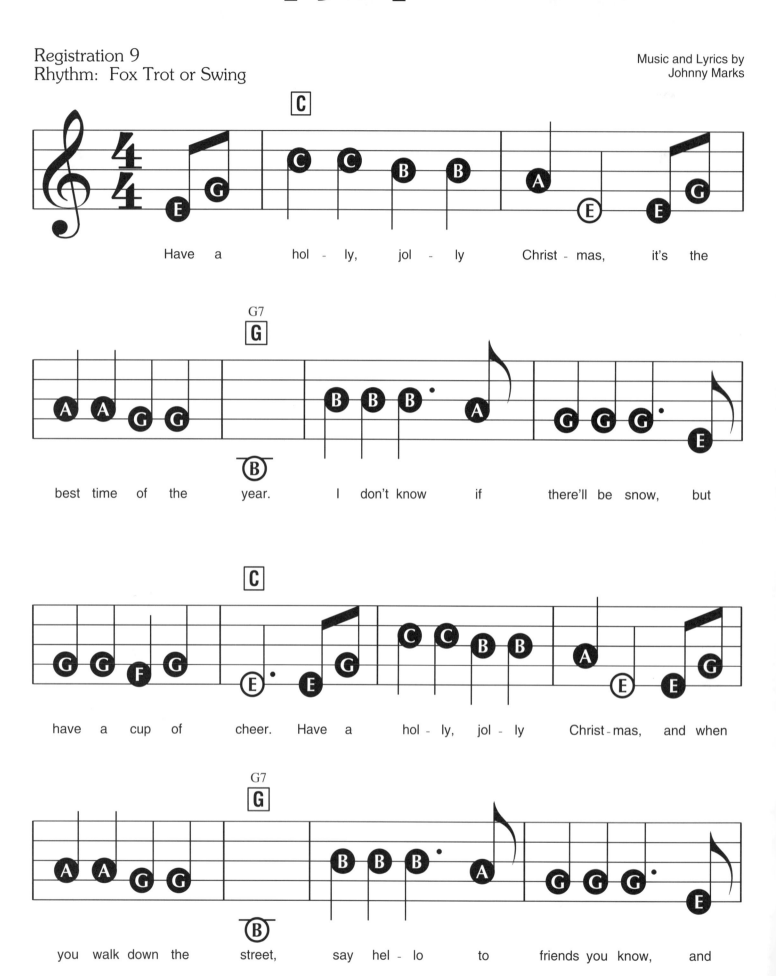

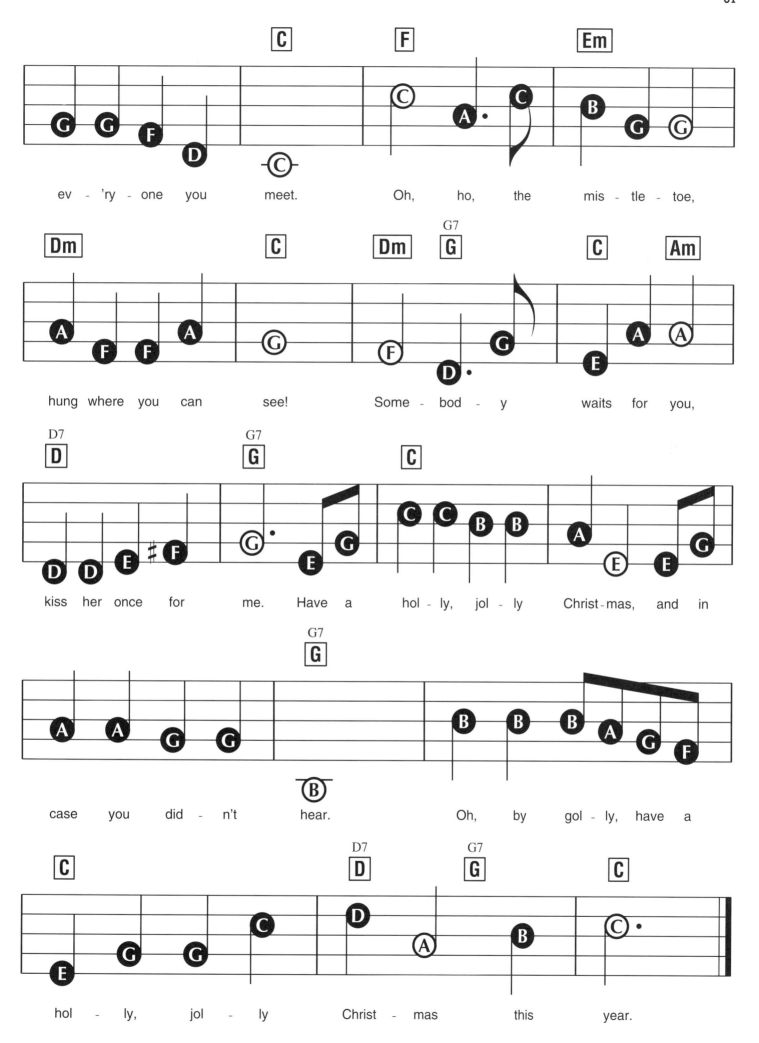

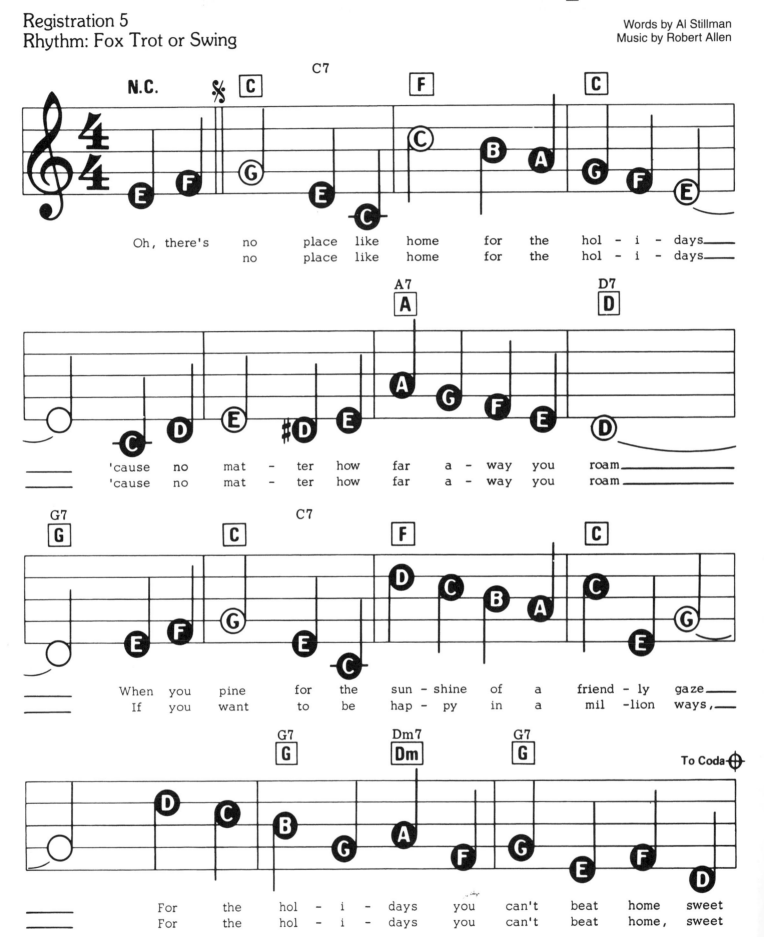

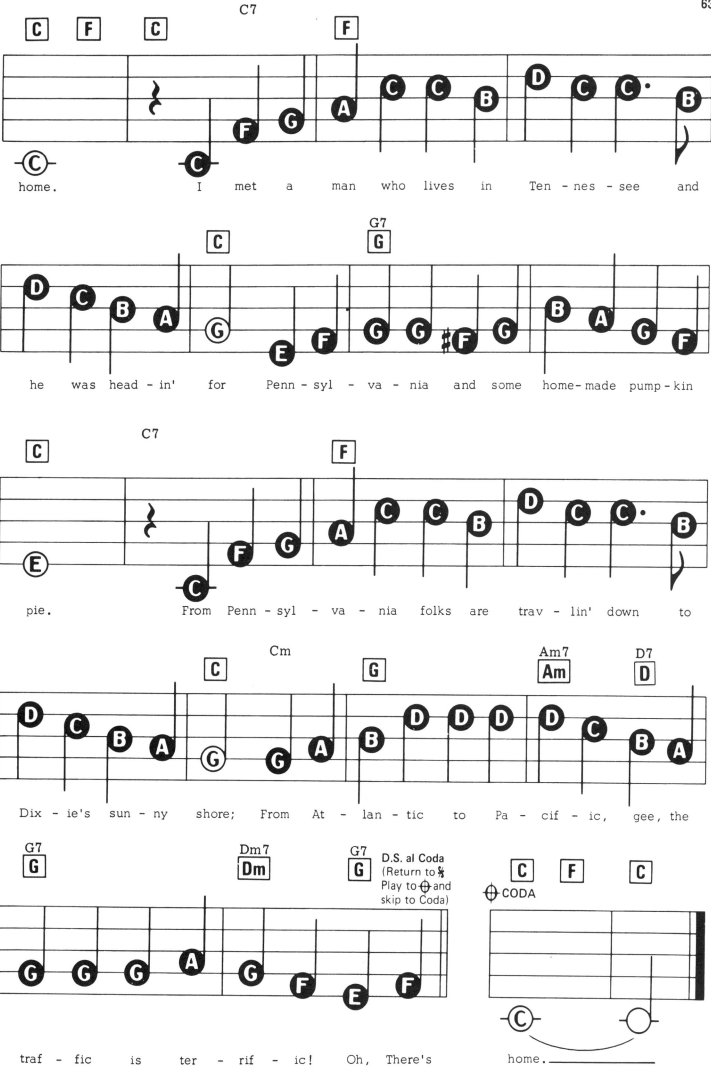

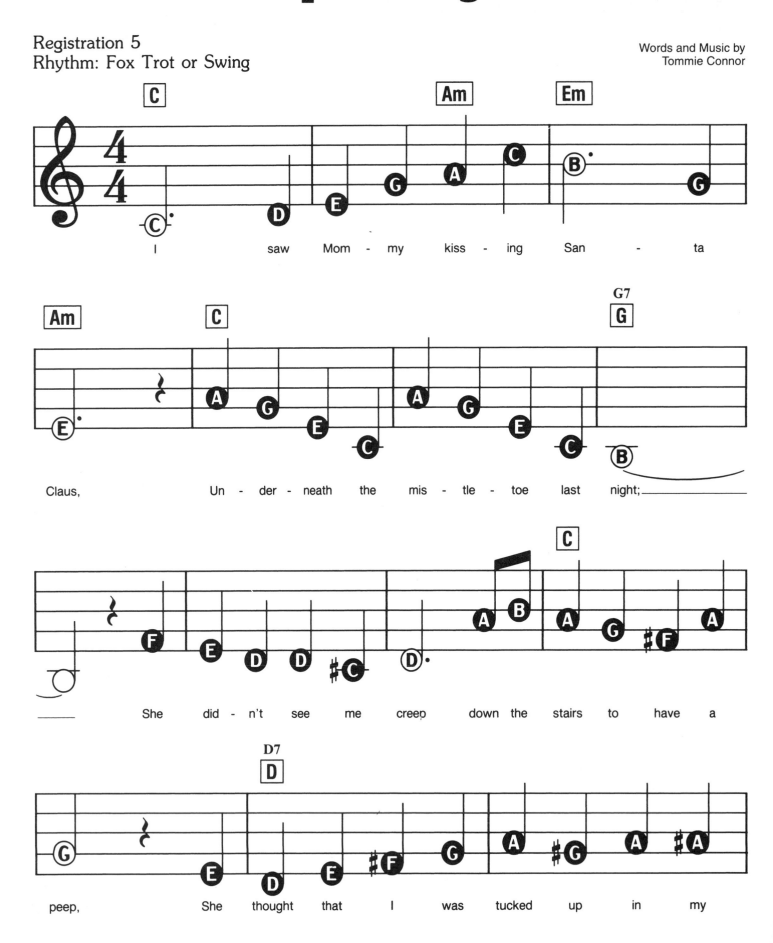

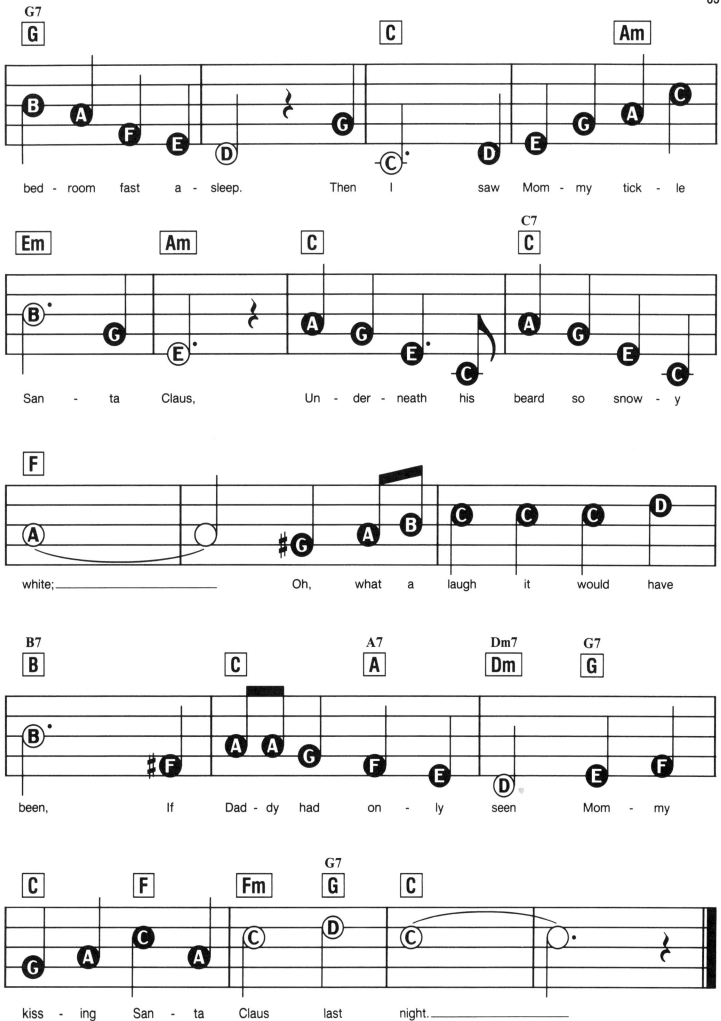

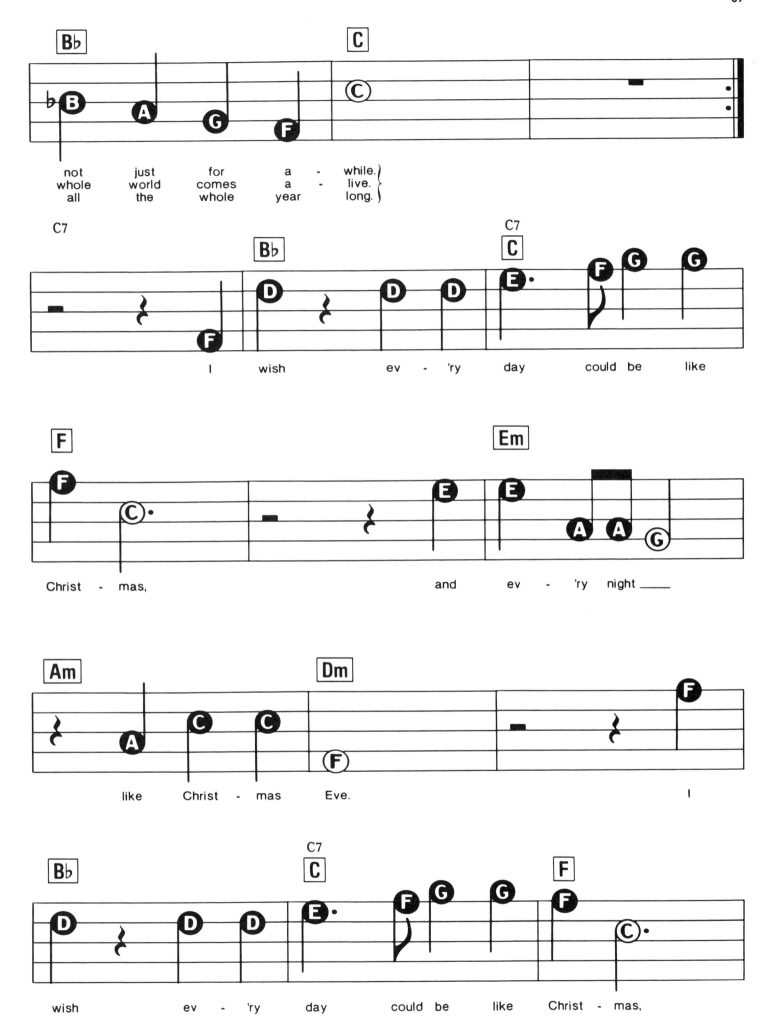

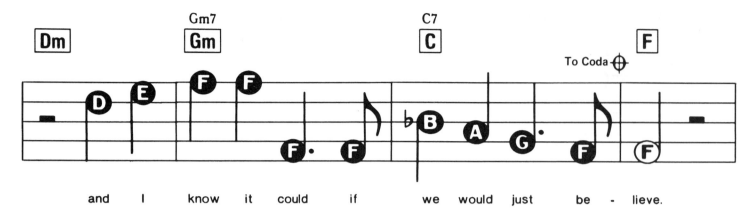
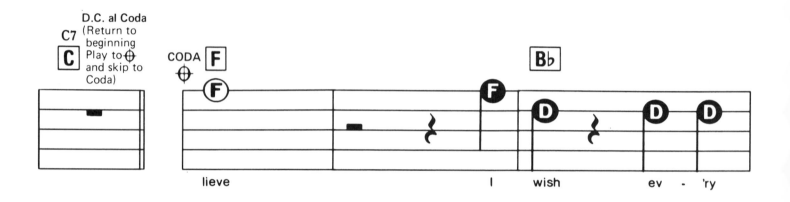
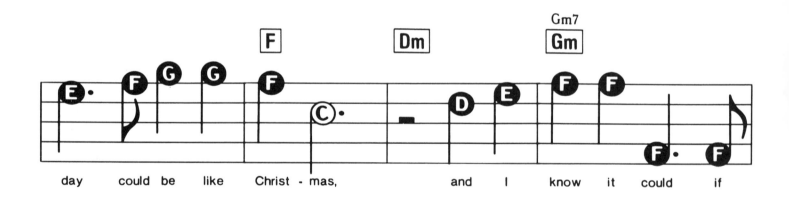
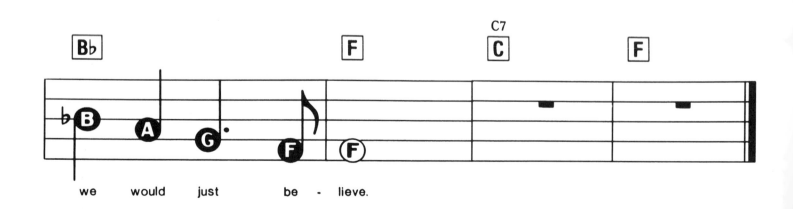

It Must Have Been the Mistletoe
(Our First Christmas)

Registration 1
Rhythm: 6/8 or Waltz

By Justin Wilde
and Doug Konecky

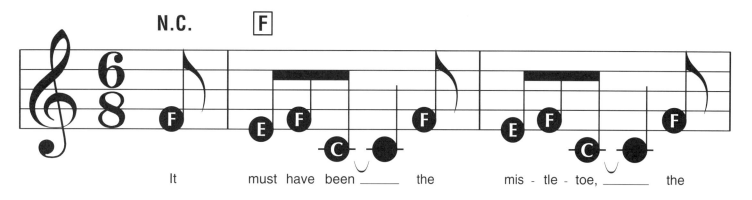

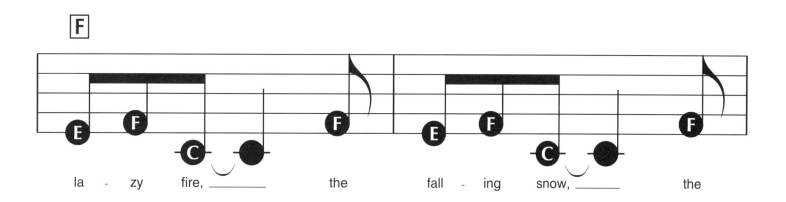

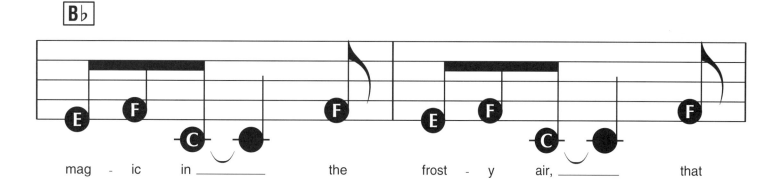

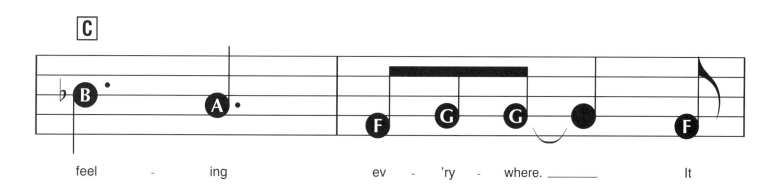

© Copyright 1979 Songcastle Music (ASCAP) and Cat's Whiskers Music (ASCAP)/both admin. by ICG
All Rights Reserved   Used by Permission

70

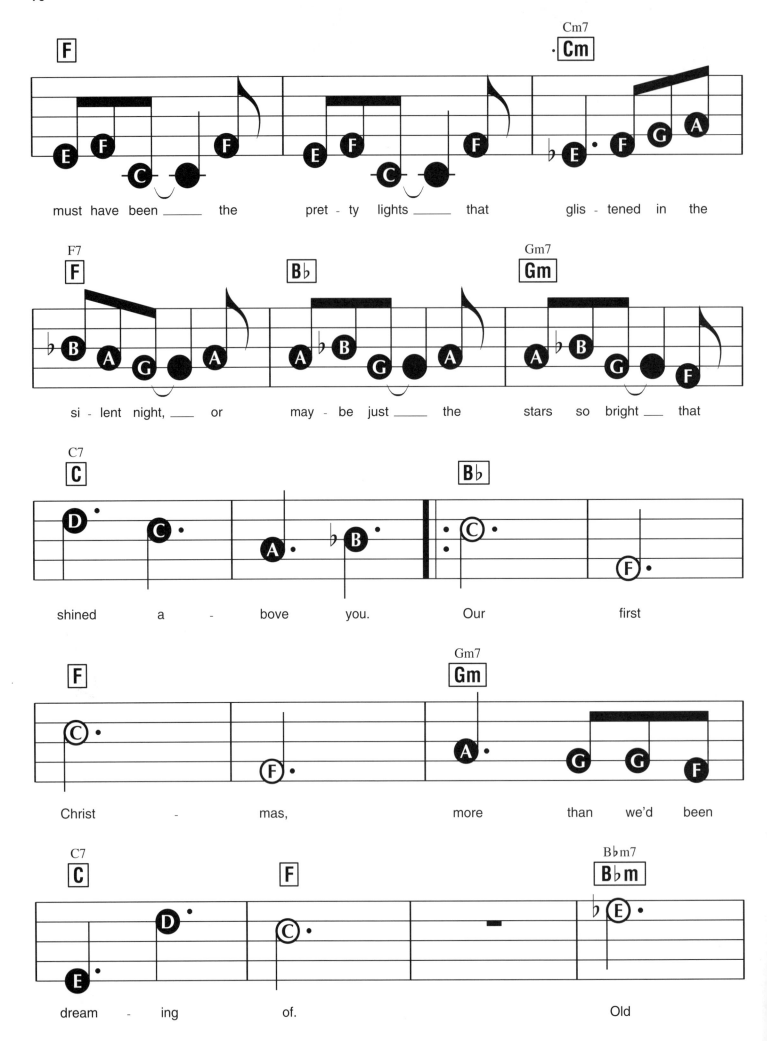

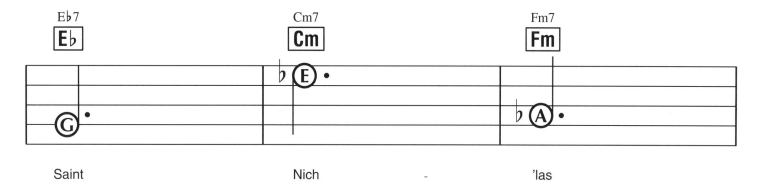
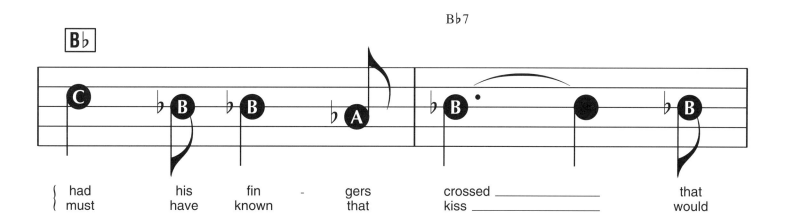
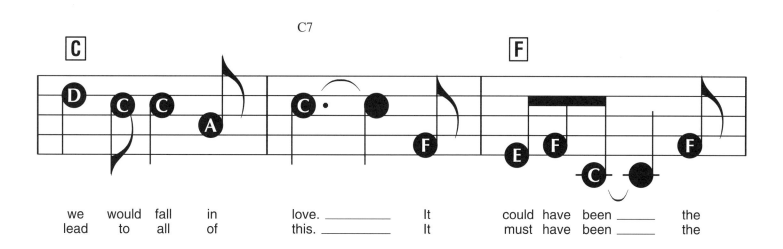
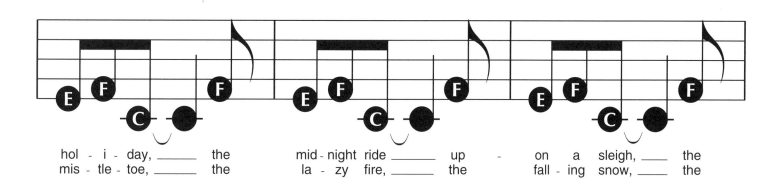

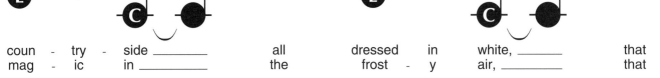
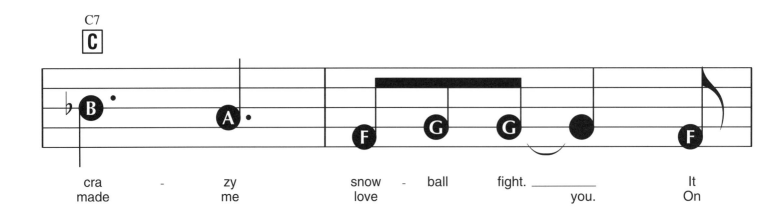
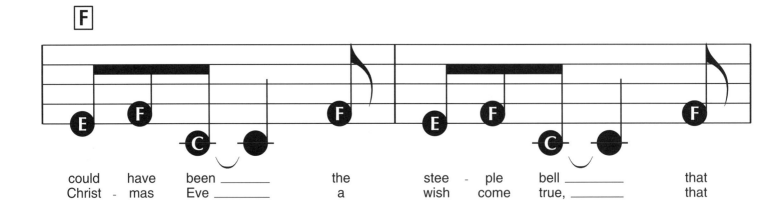
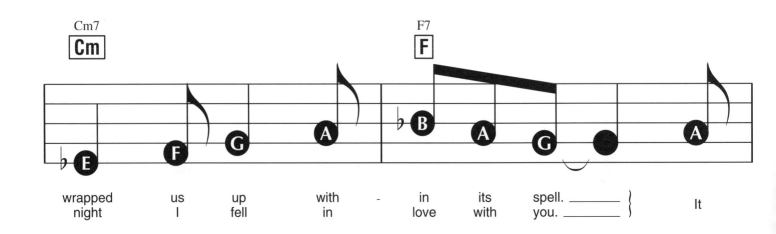

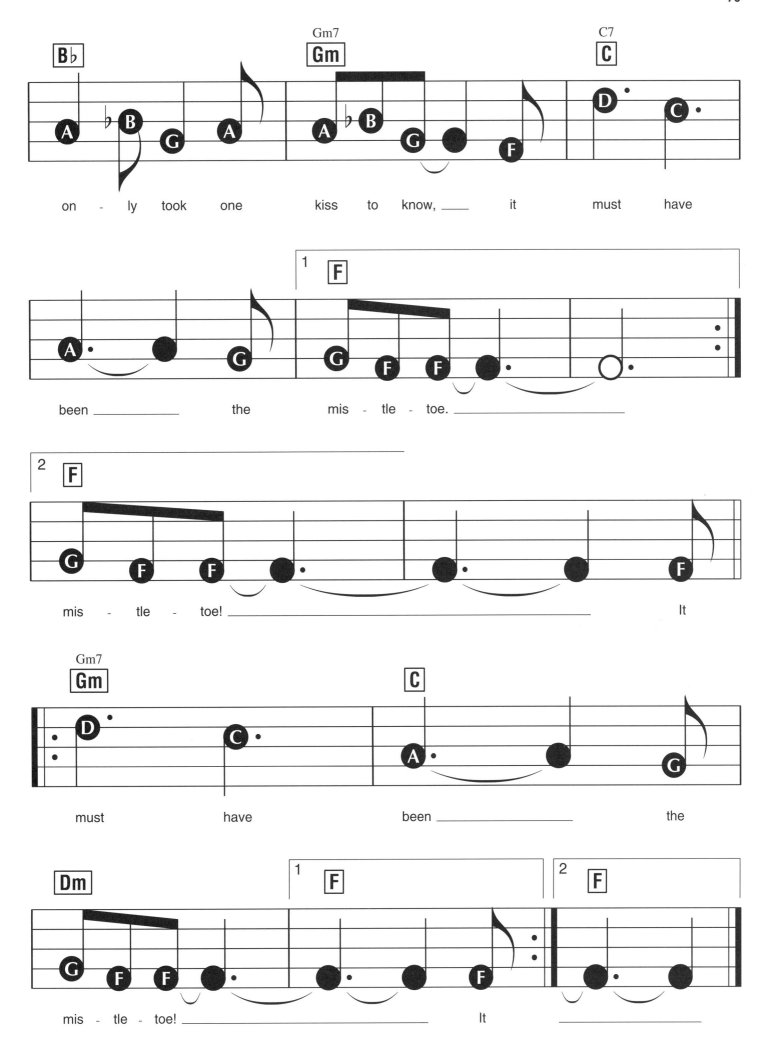

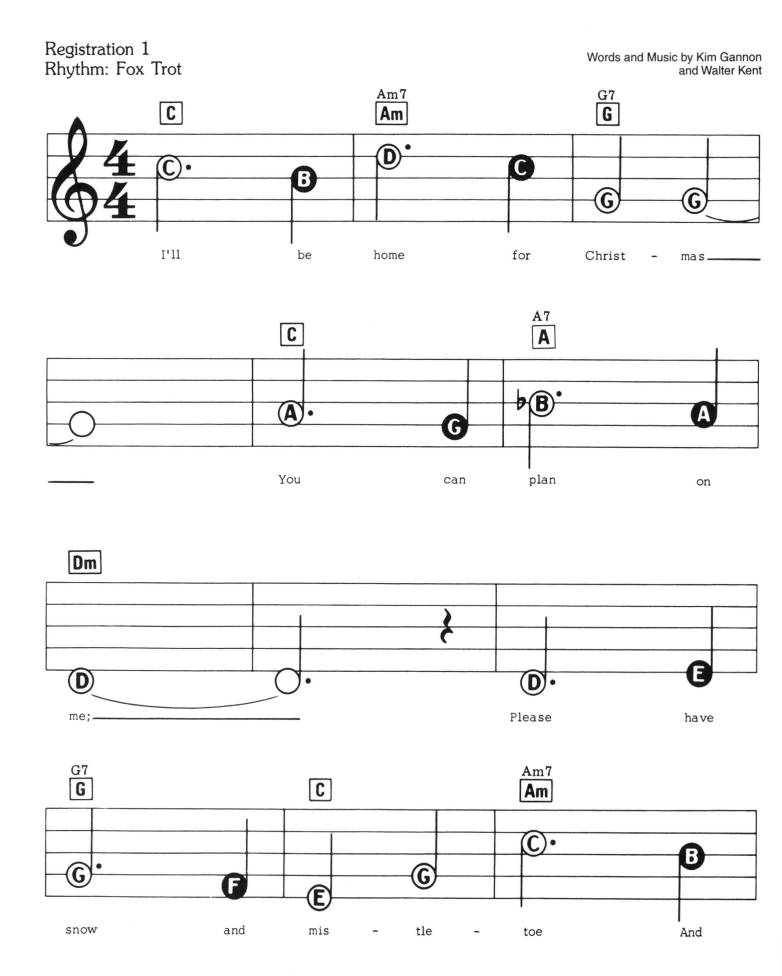

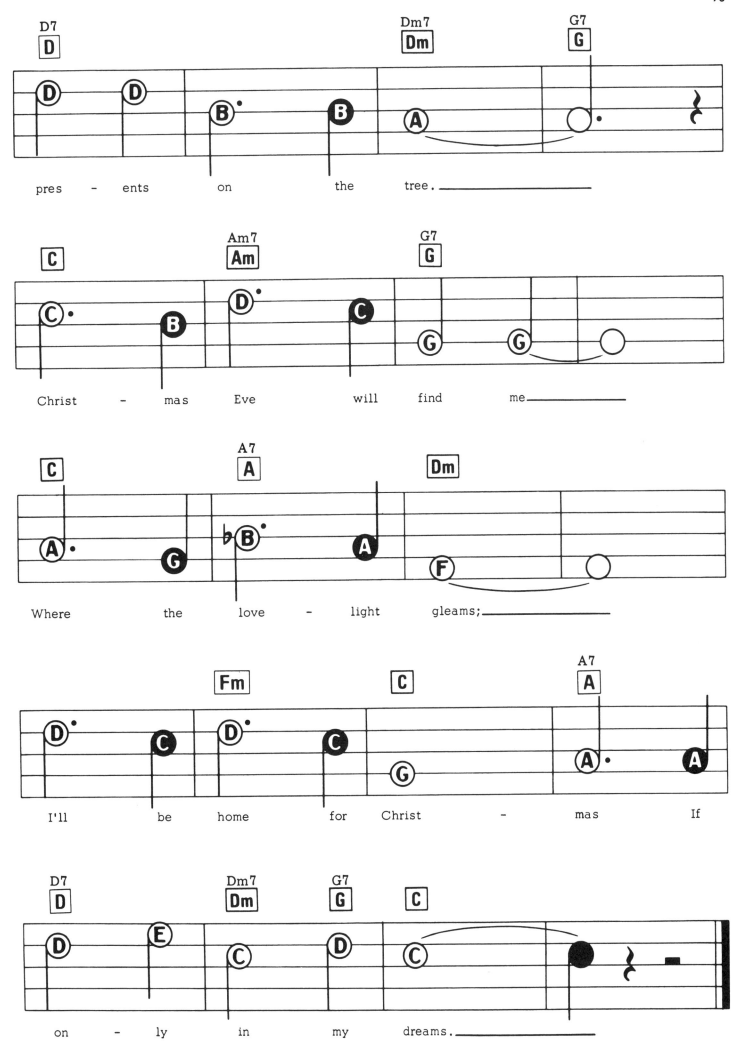

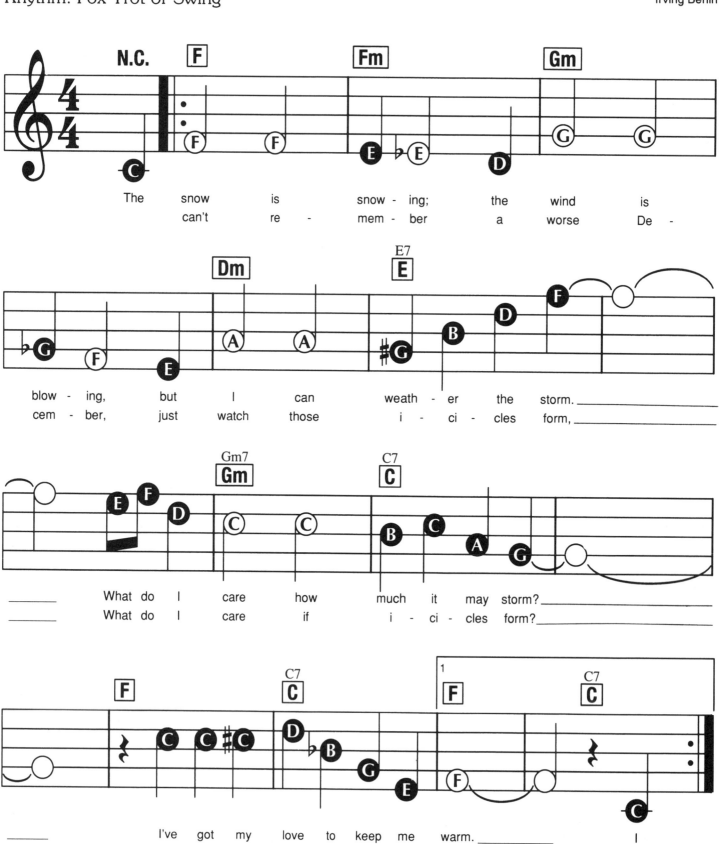

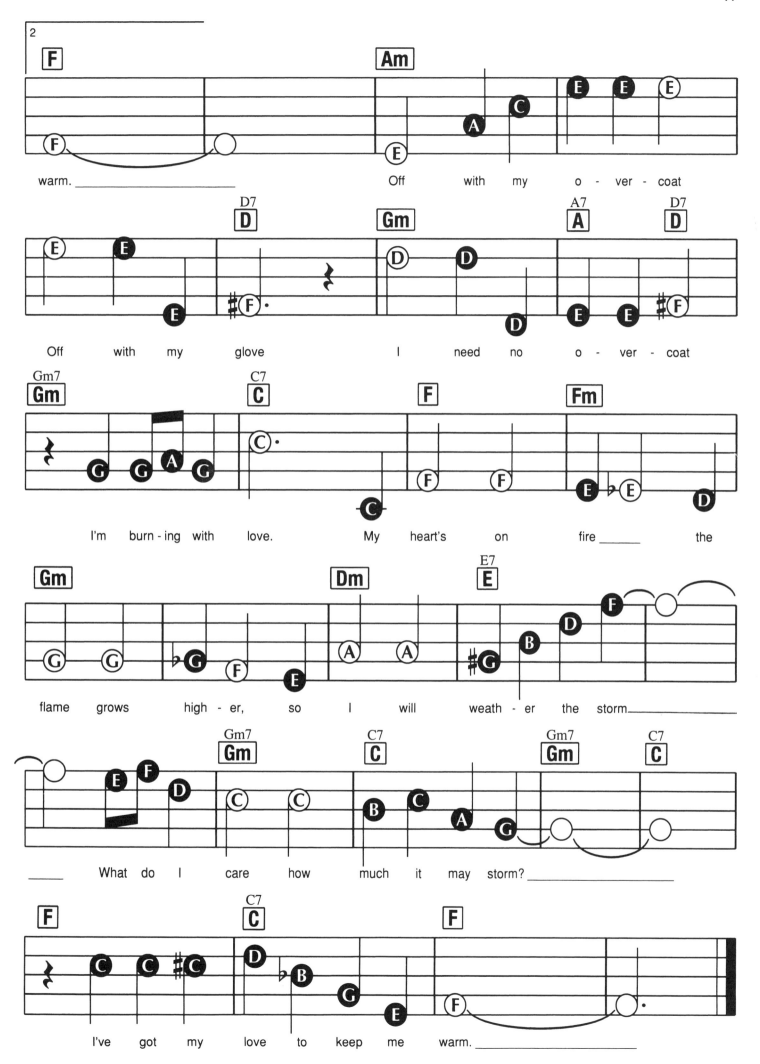

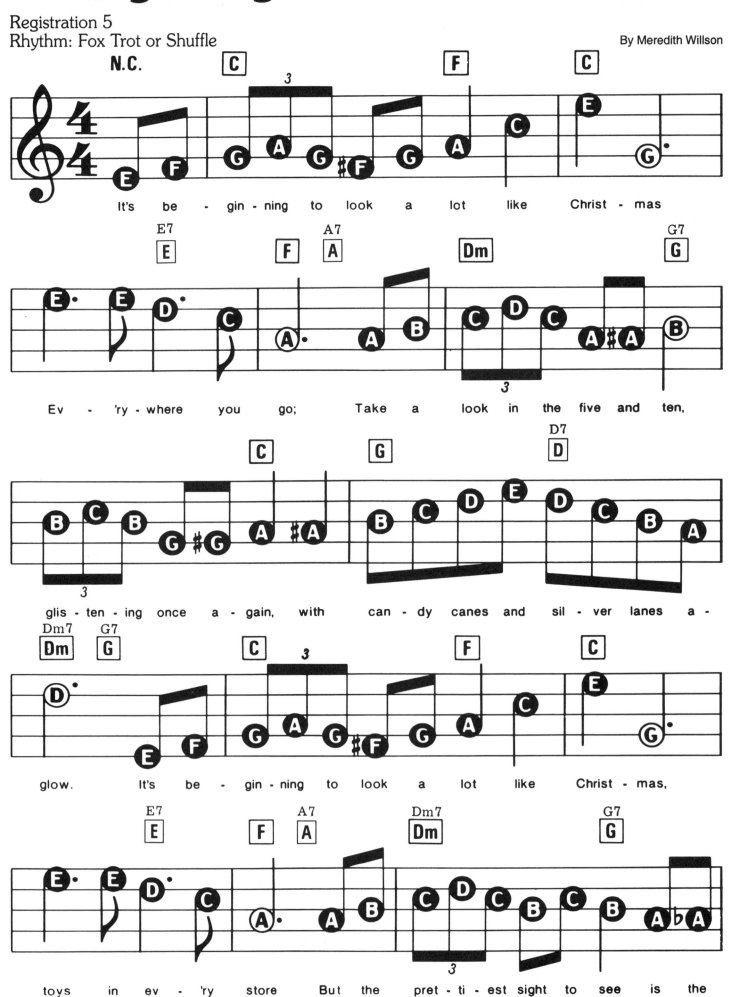

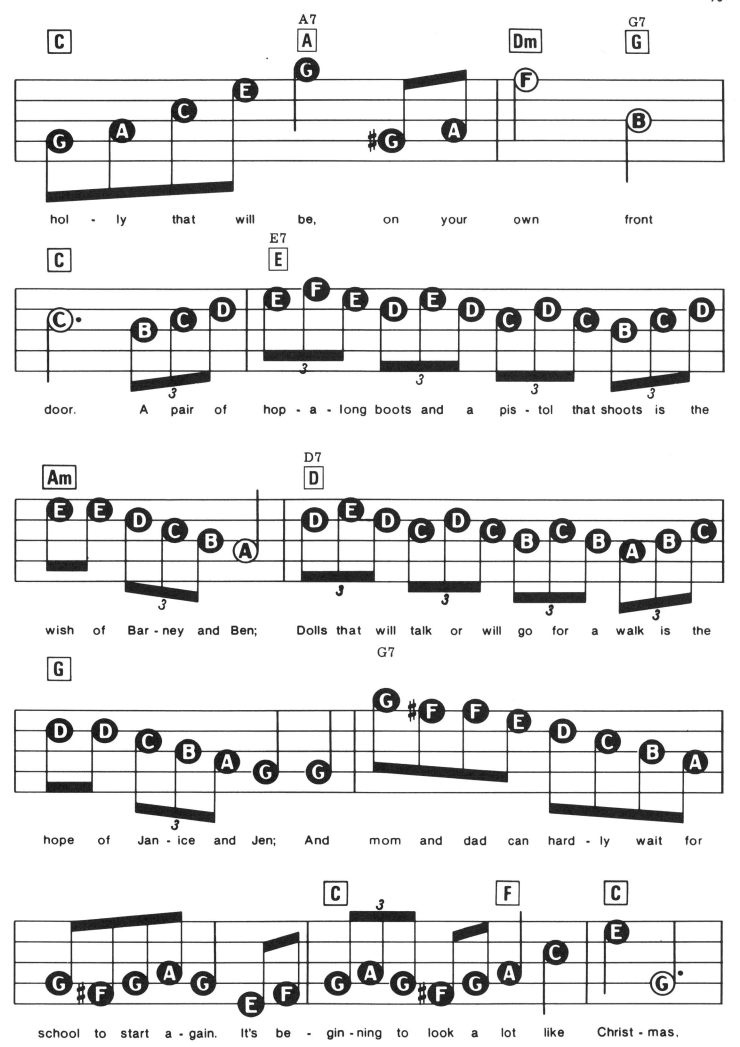

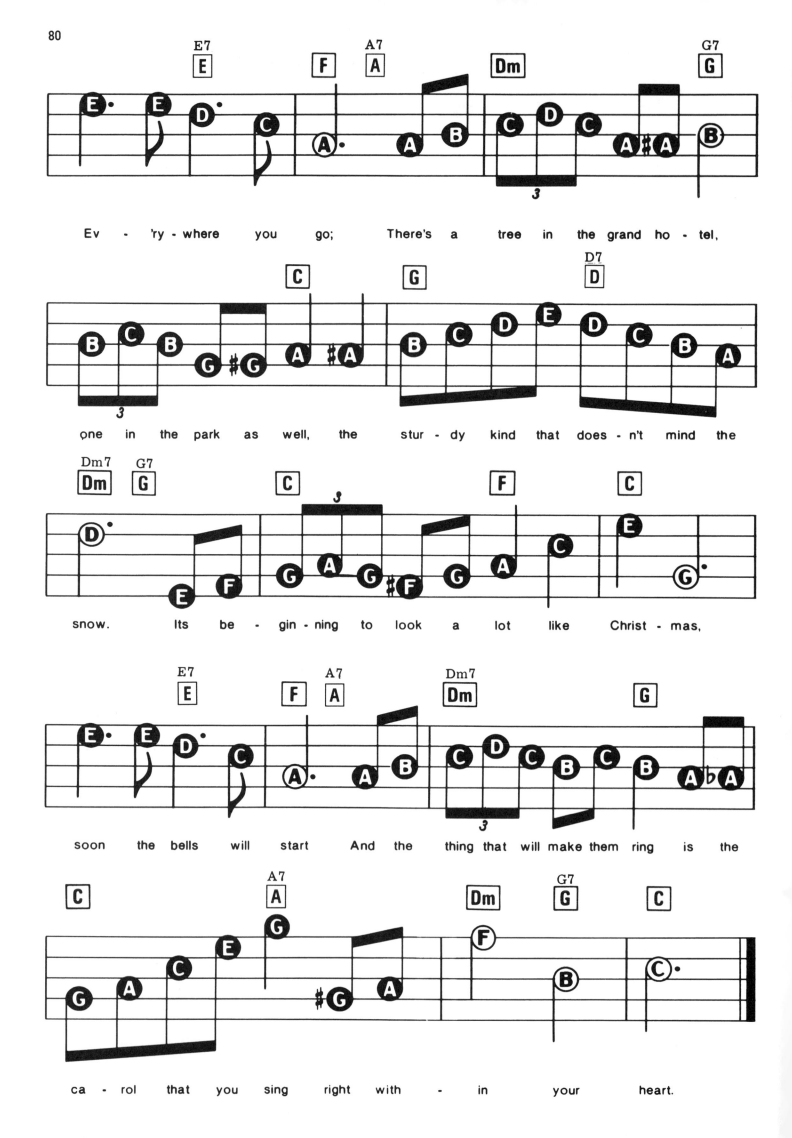

Jingle-Bell Rock

Registration 5
Rhythm: Fox Trot or Swing

Words and Music by Joe Beal
and Jim Boothe

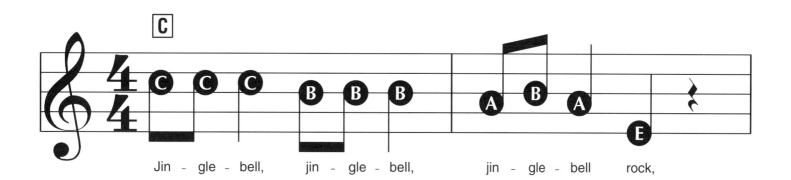
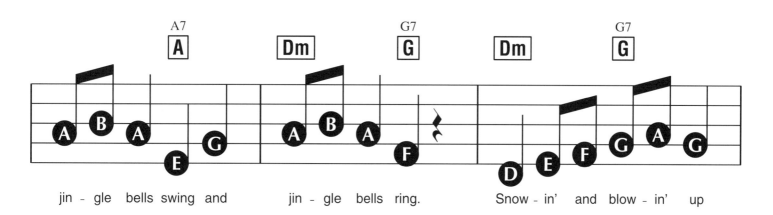
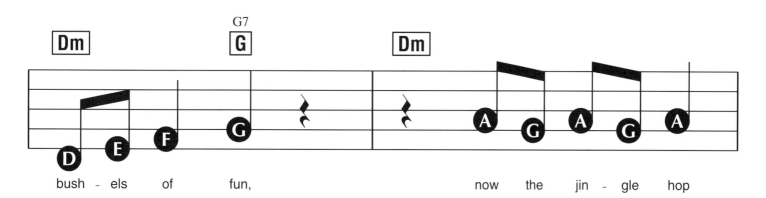
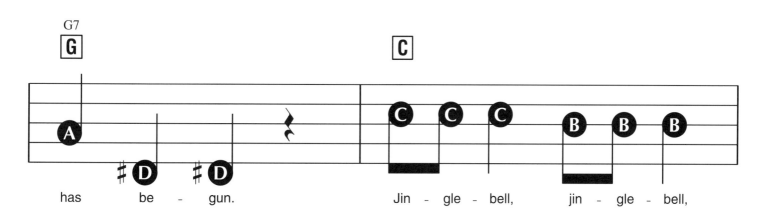

Copyright © 1957 by Chappell & Co.
Copyright Renewed
International Copyright Secured   All Rights Reserved

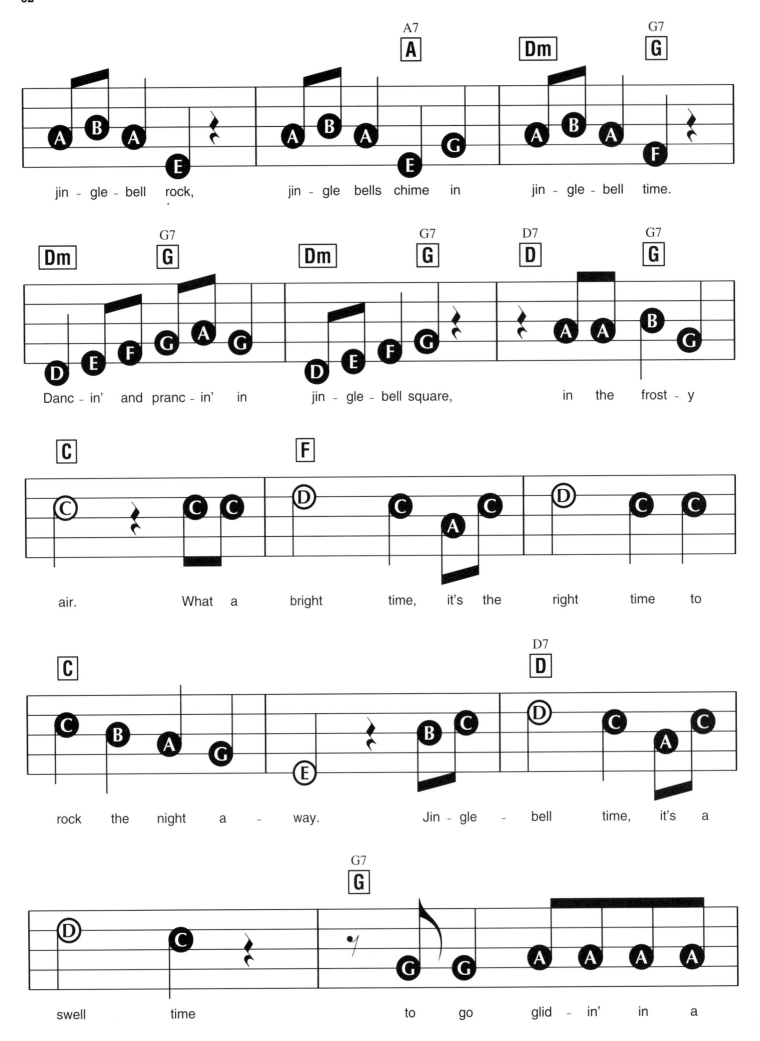

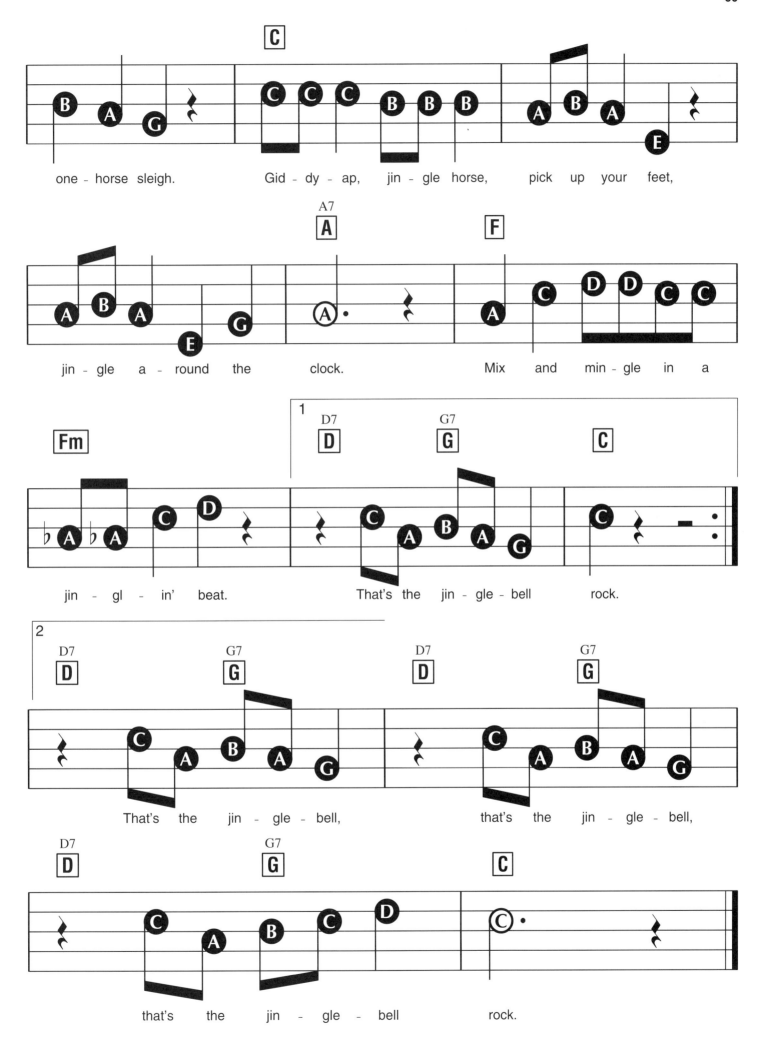

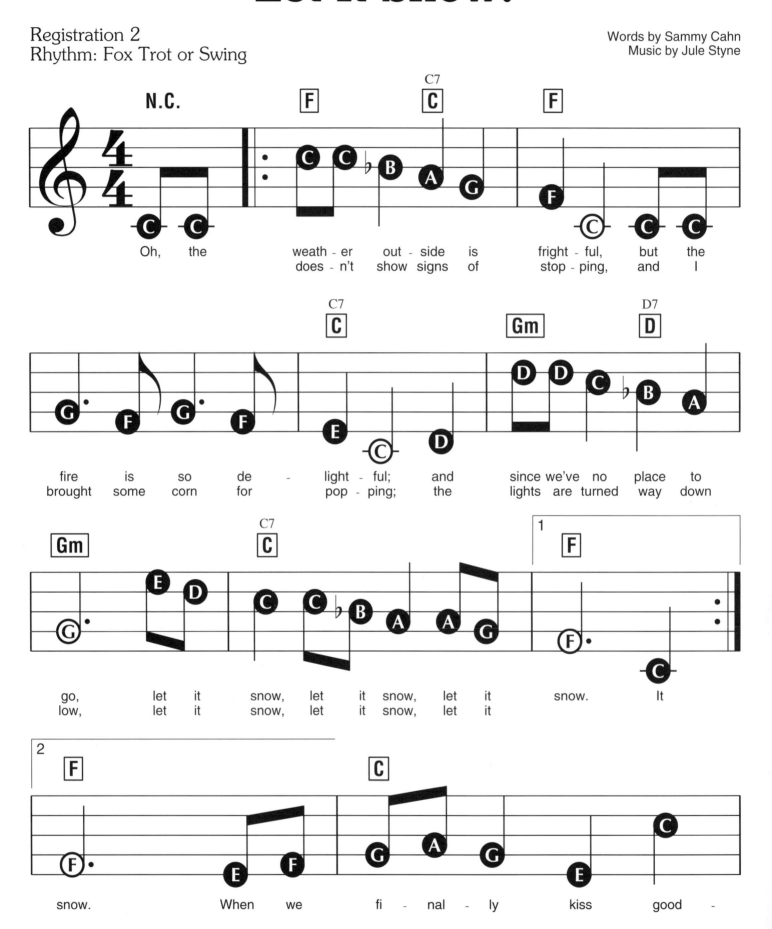

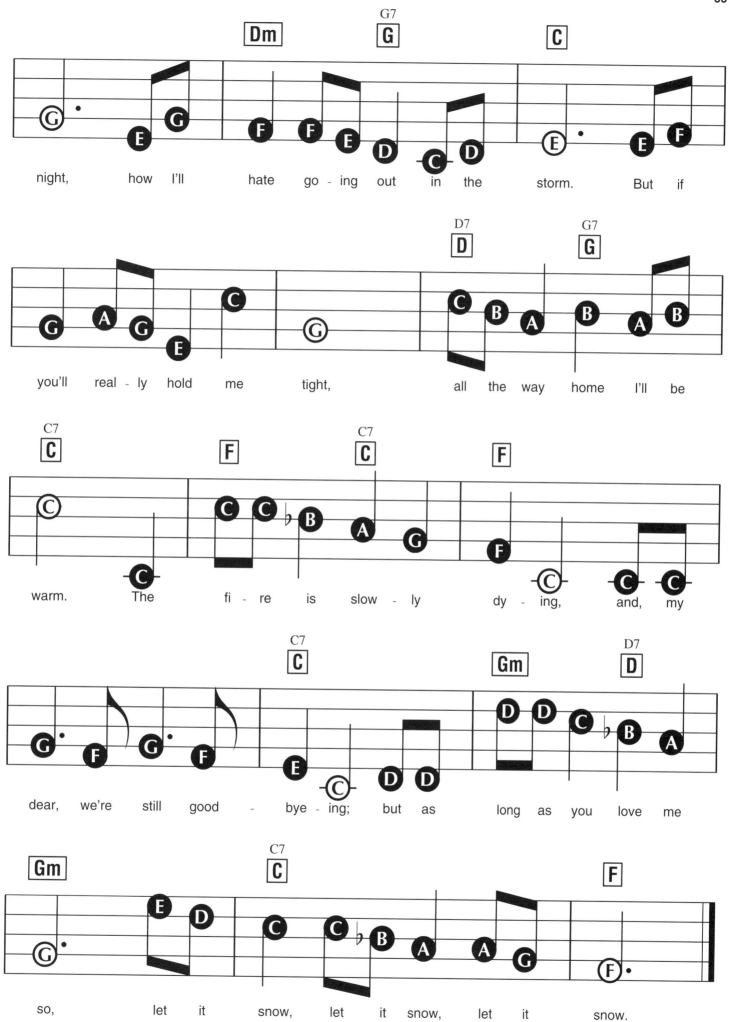

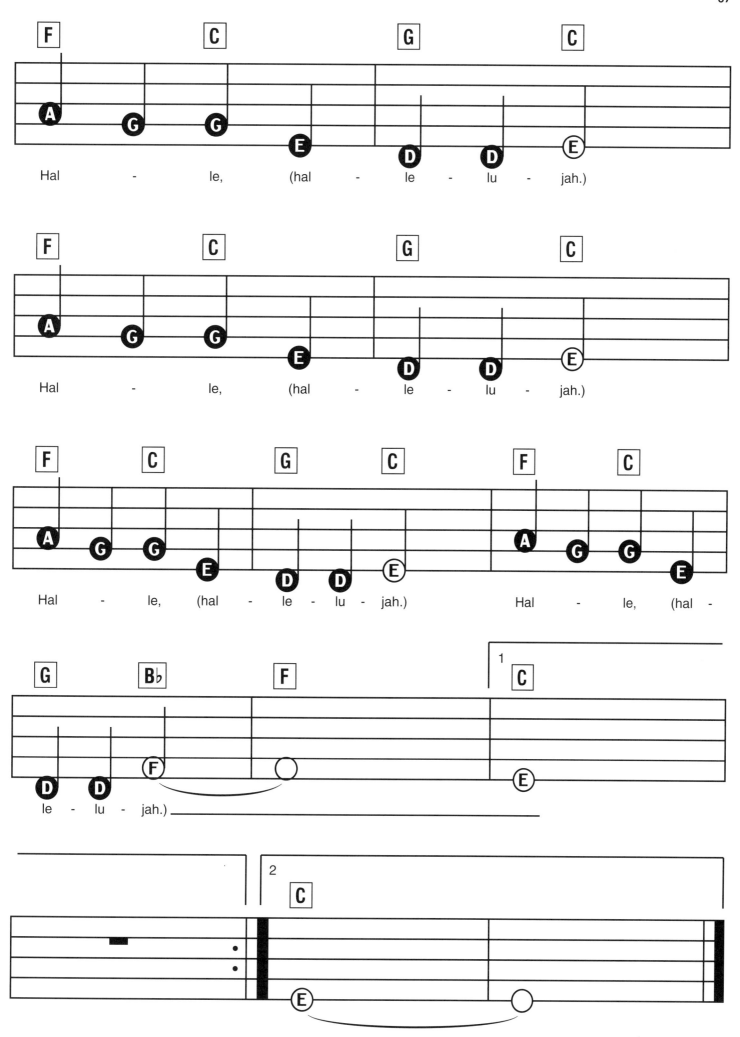

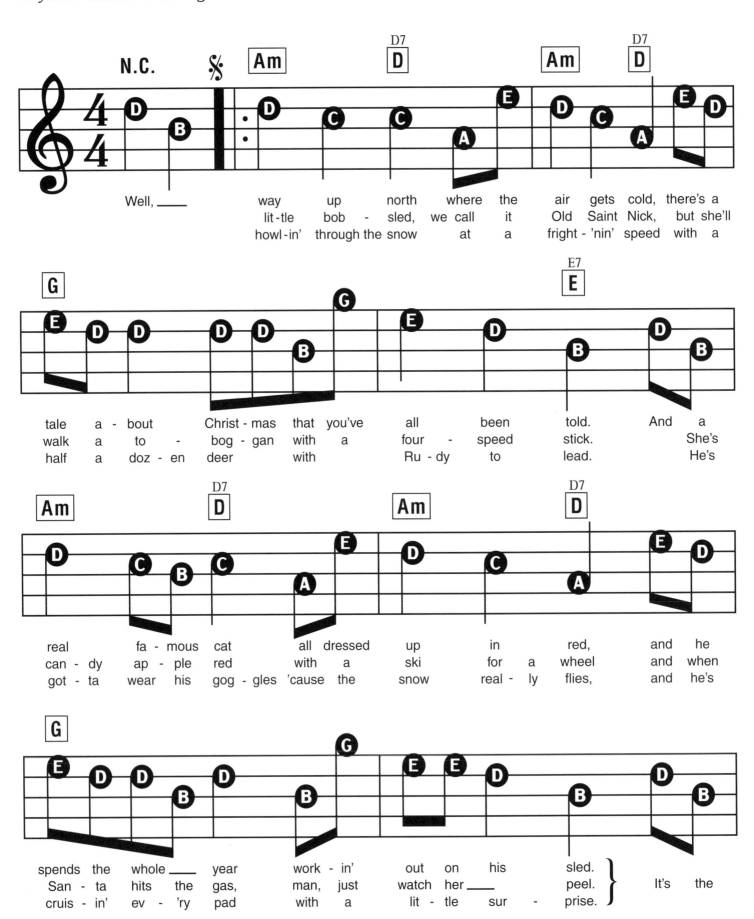

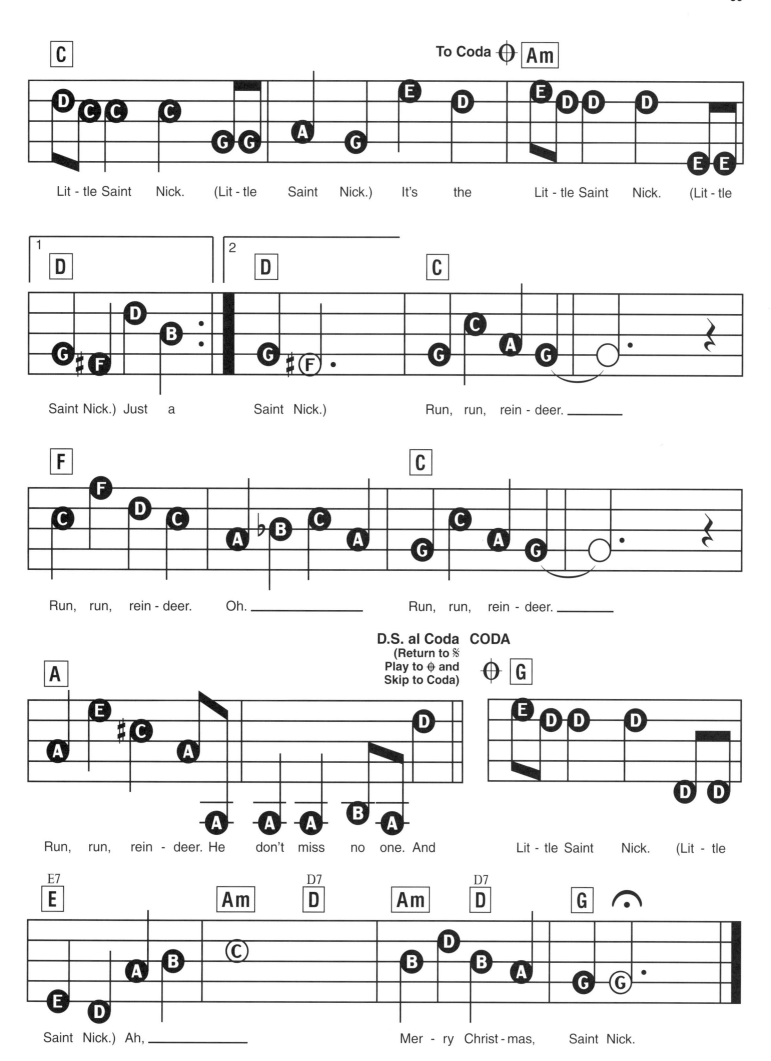

A Marshmallow World

Registration 2
Rhythm: Fox Trot or Swing

Words by Carl Sigman
Music by Peter De Rose

Copyright © 1949, 1950 Shapiro, Bernstein & Co., Inc., New York
Copyright Renewed
International Copyright Secured   All Rights Reserved
Used by Permission

Merry Christmas, Darling

Registration 9
Rhythm: 4/4 Ballad

Words and Music by Richard Carpenter
and Frank Pooler

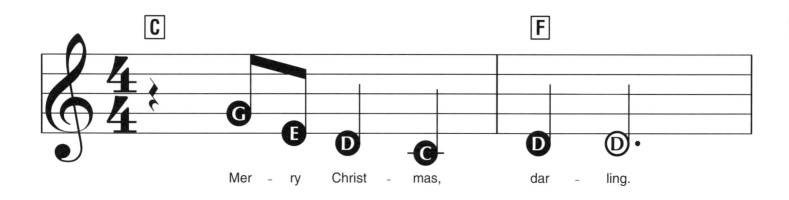

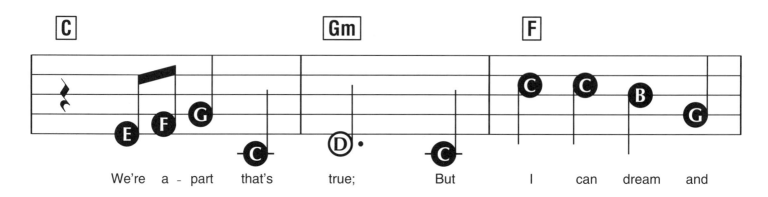

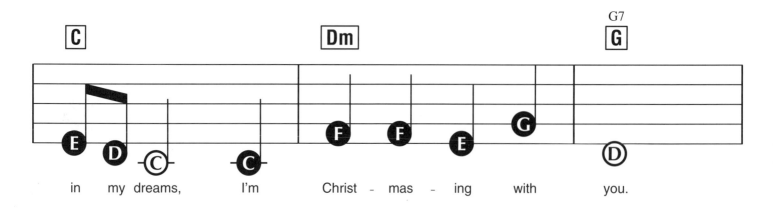

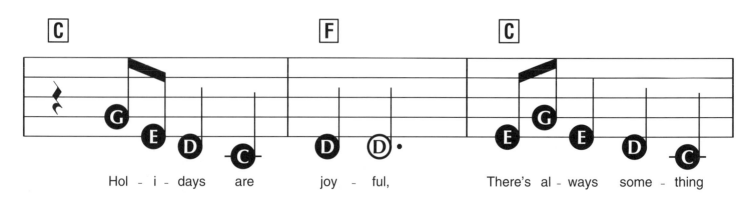

Copyright © 1970 IRVING MUSIC, INC.
Copyright Renewed
All Rights Reserved   Used by Permission

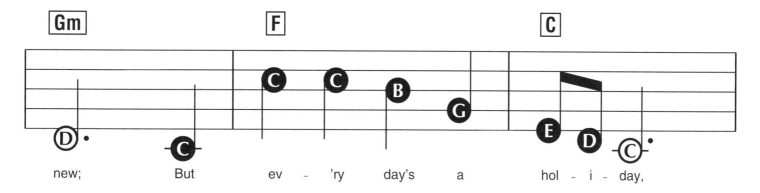
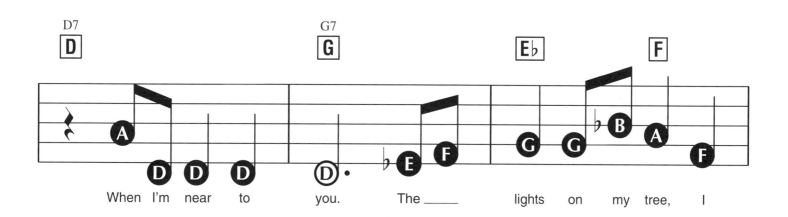
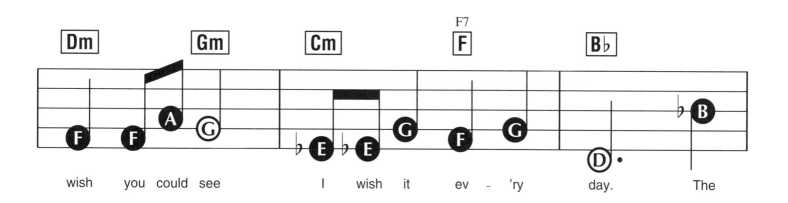
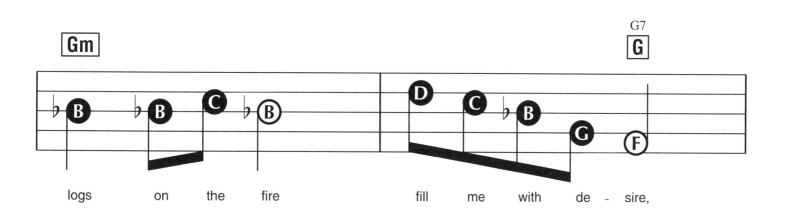

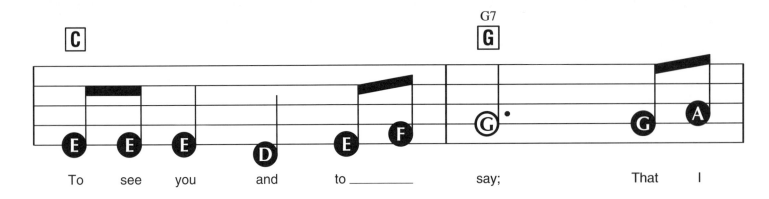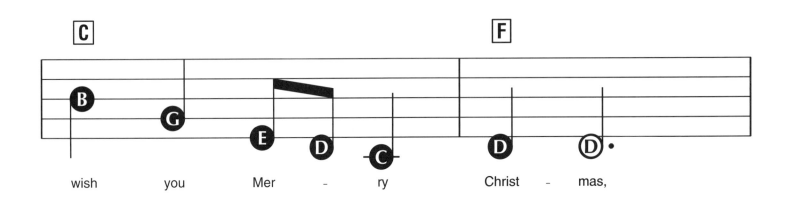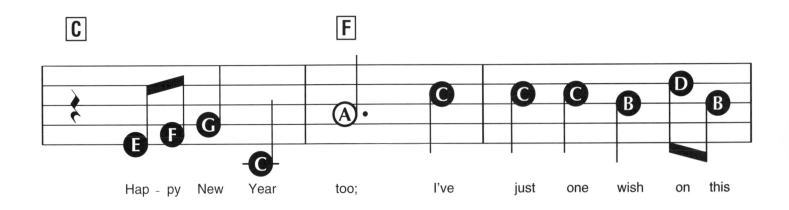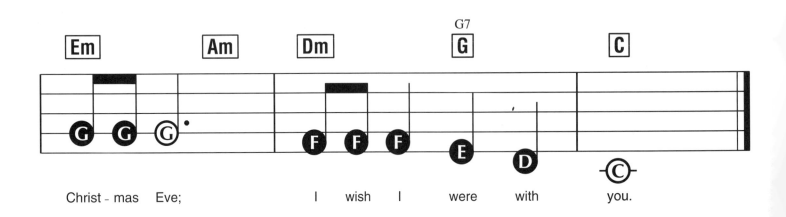

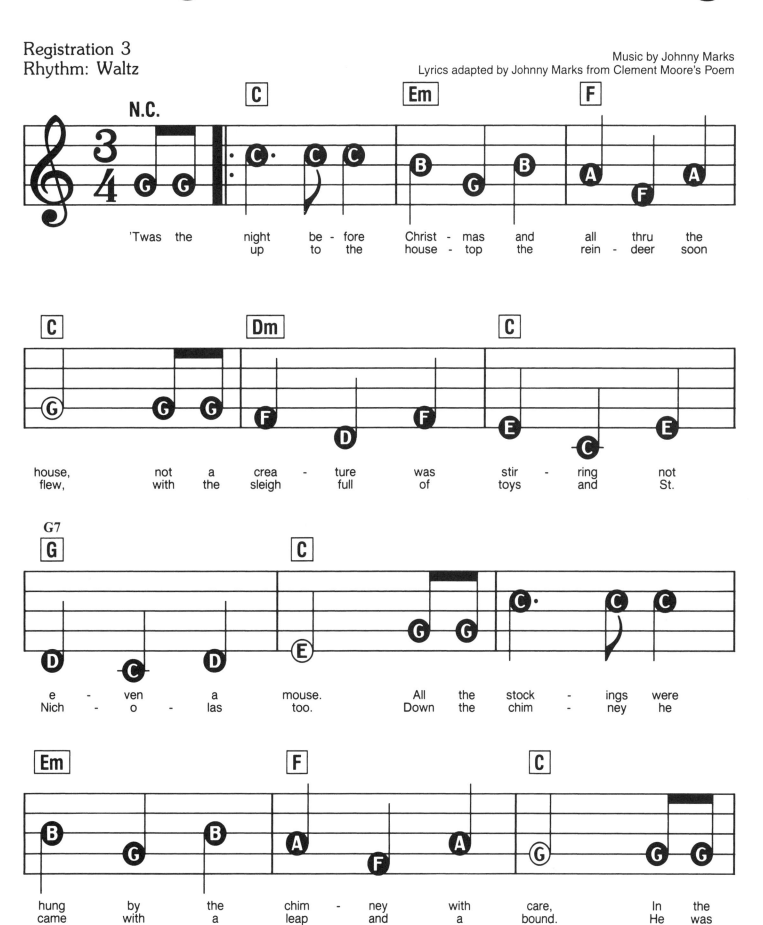

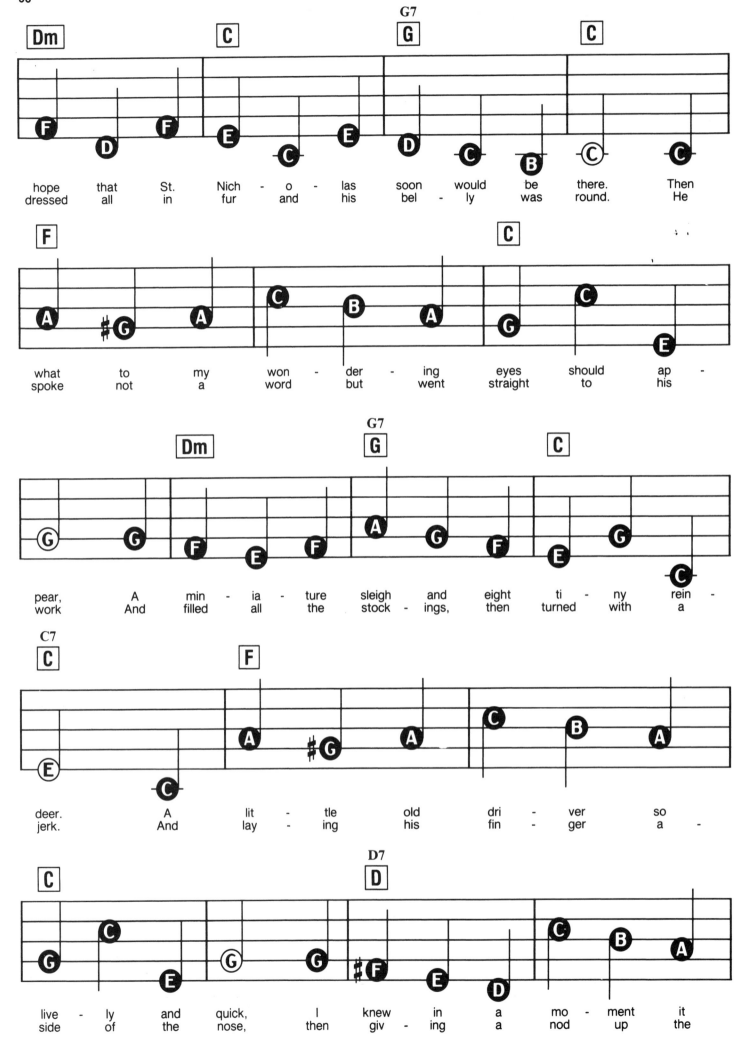

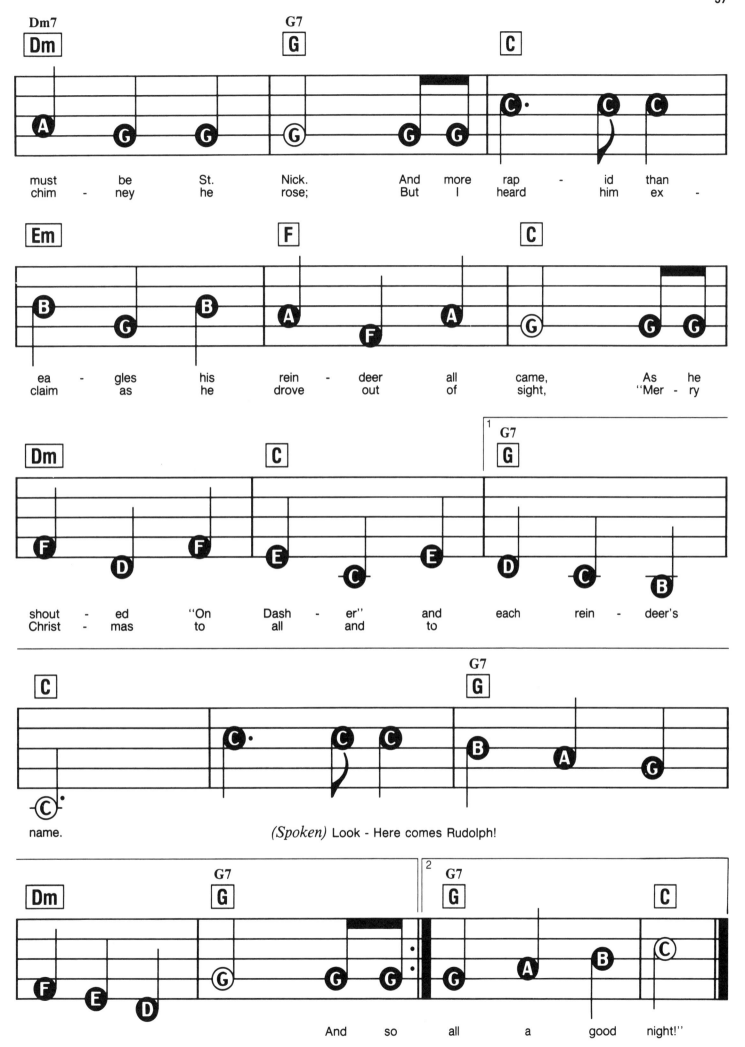

Merry Christmas Waltz

Registration 4
Rhythm: Waltz

Words and Music by Bob Batson
and Inex Loewer

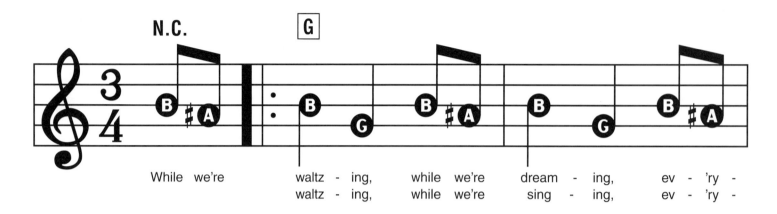

While we're waltz-ing, while we're dream-ing, ev-'ry-
waltz-ing, while we're sing-ing, ev-'ry-

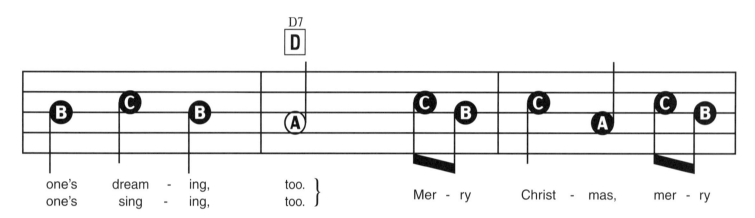

one's dream-ing, too. } Mer-ry Christ-mas, mer-ry
one's sing-ing, too.

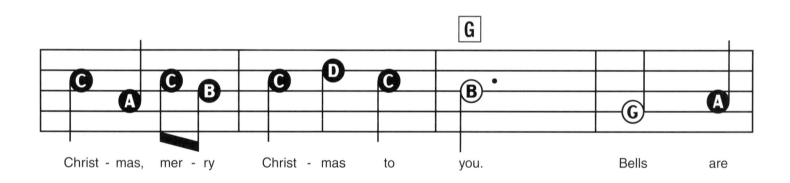

Christ-mas, mer-ry Christ-mas to you. Bells are

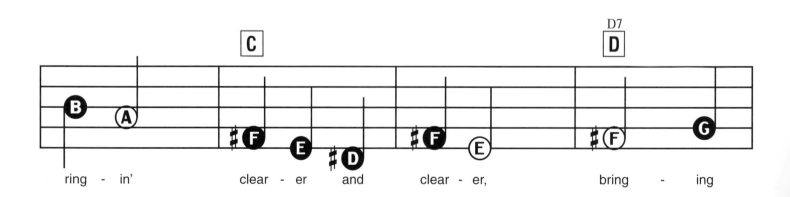

ring-in' clear-er and clear-er, bring-ing

© 1955 (Renewed) Golden West Melodies, Inc.
All Rights Reserved   Used by Permission

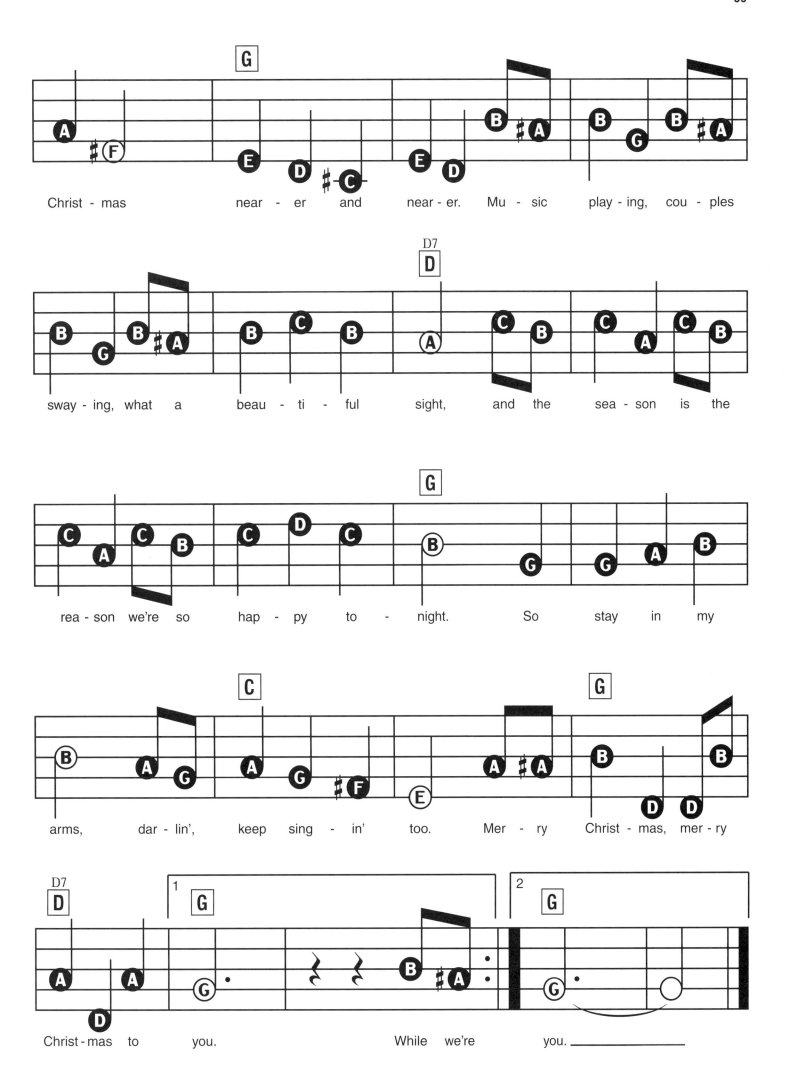

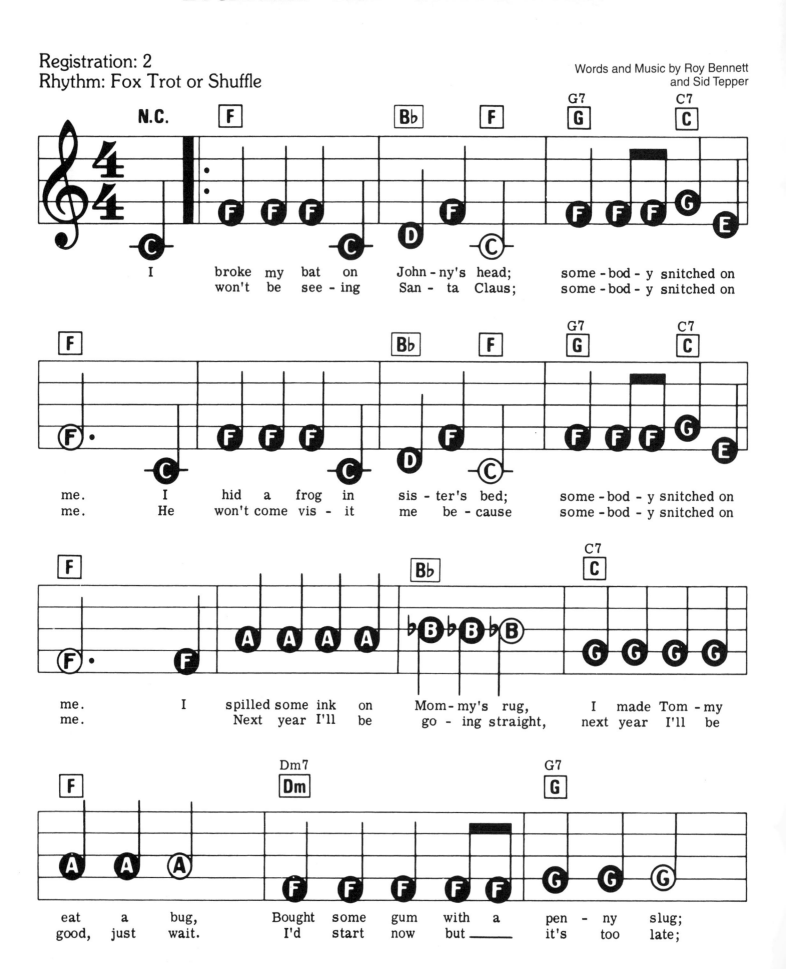

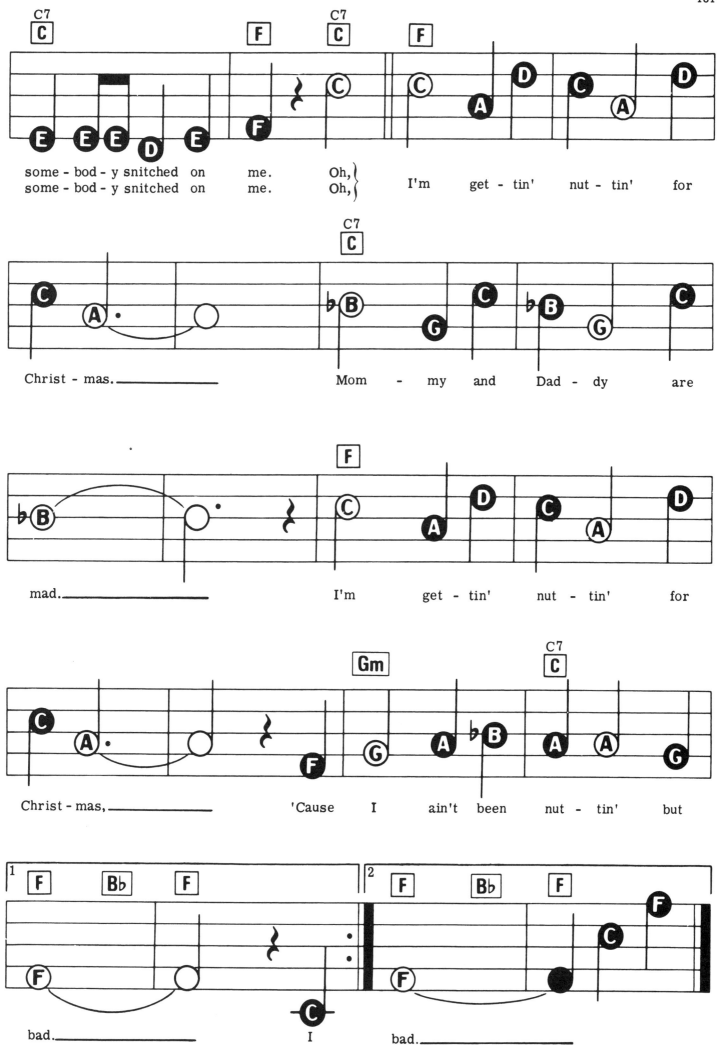

Rudolph the Red-Nosed Reindeer

Registration 4
Rhythm: Fox Trot or Swing

Music and Lyrics by
Johnny Marks

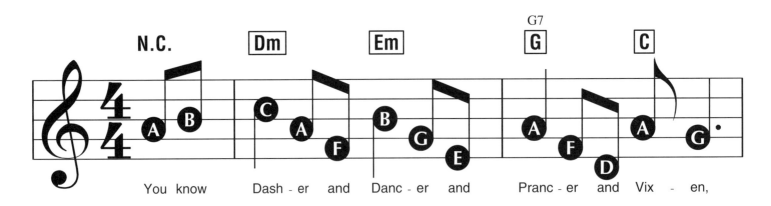

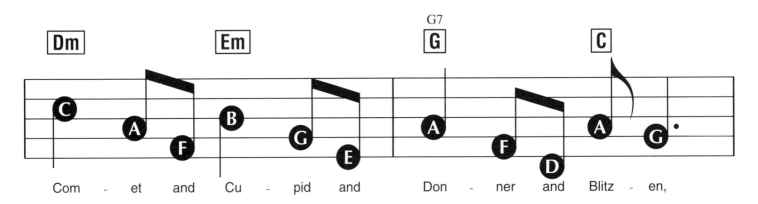

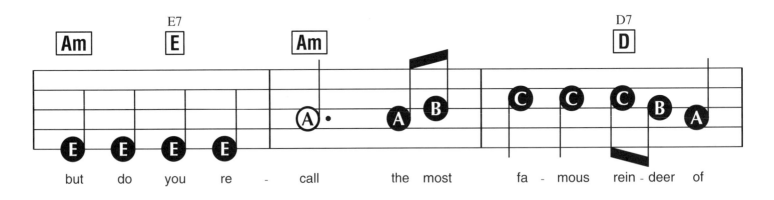

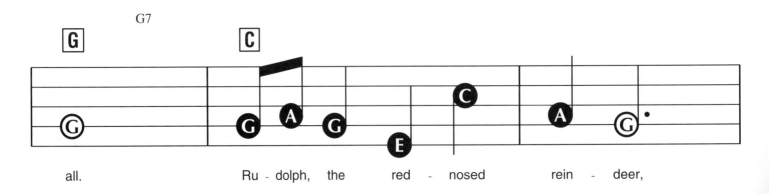

Copyright © 1949 (Renewed 1977) St. Nicholas Music Inc., 1619 Broadway, New York, New York 10019
All Rights Reserved

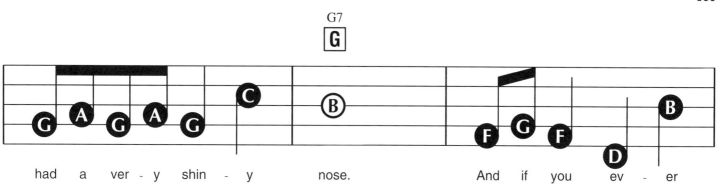
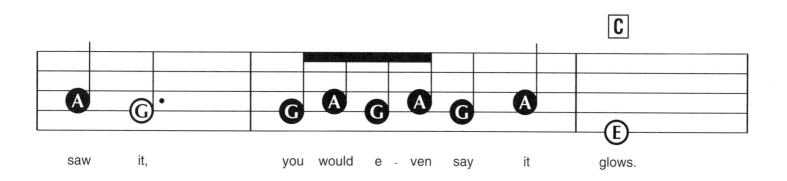
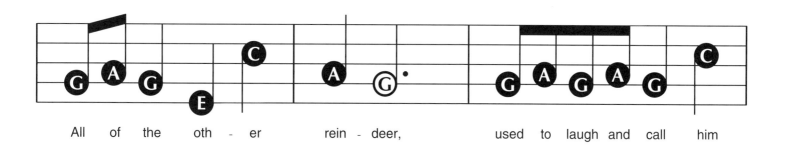
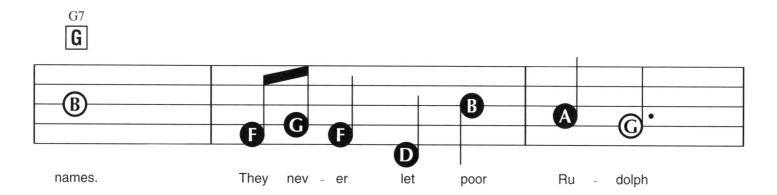
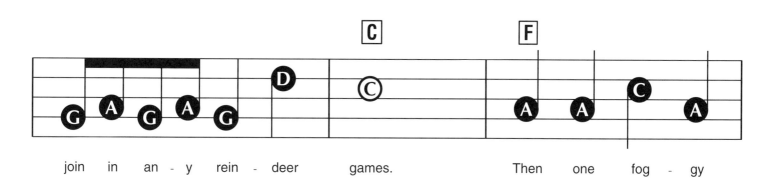

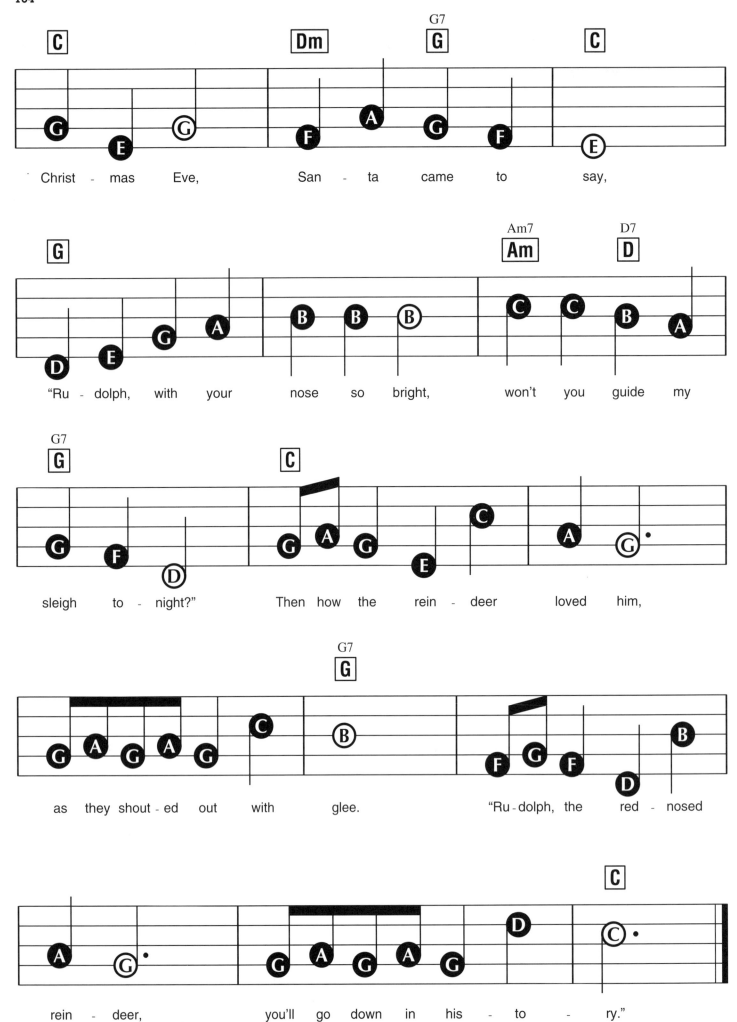

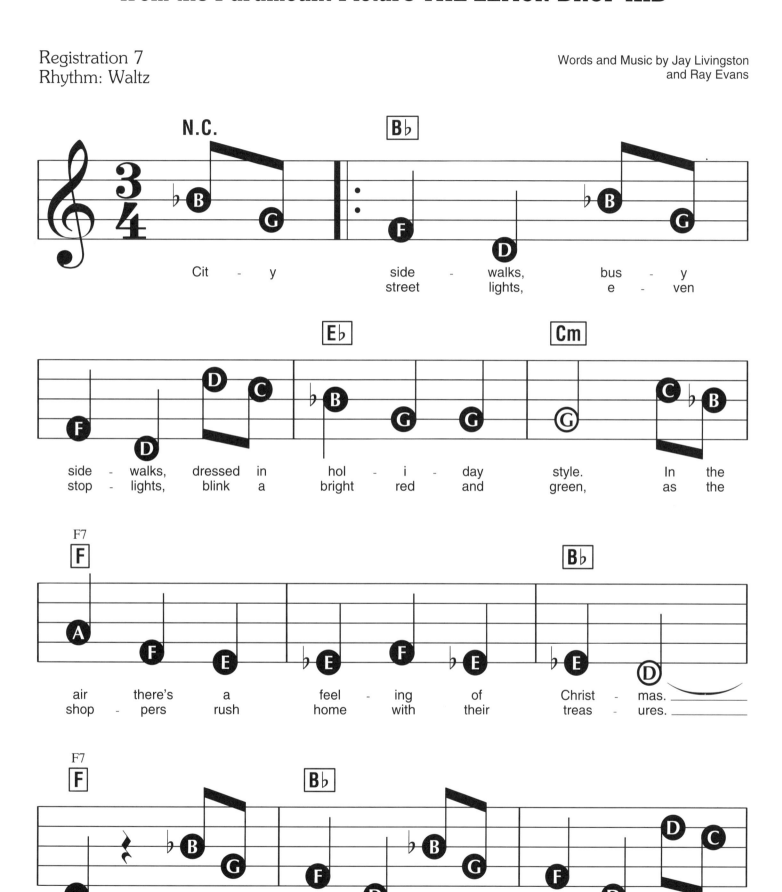

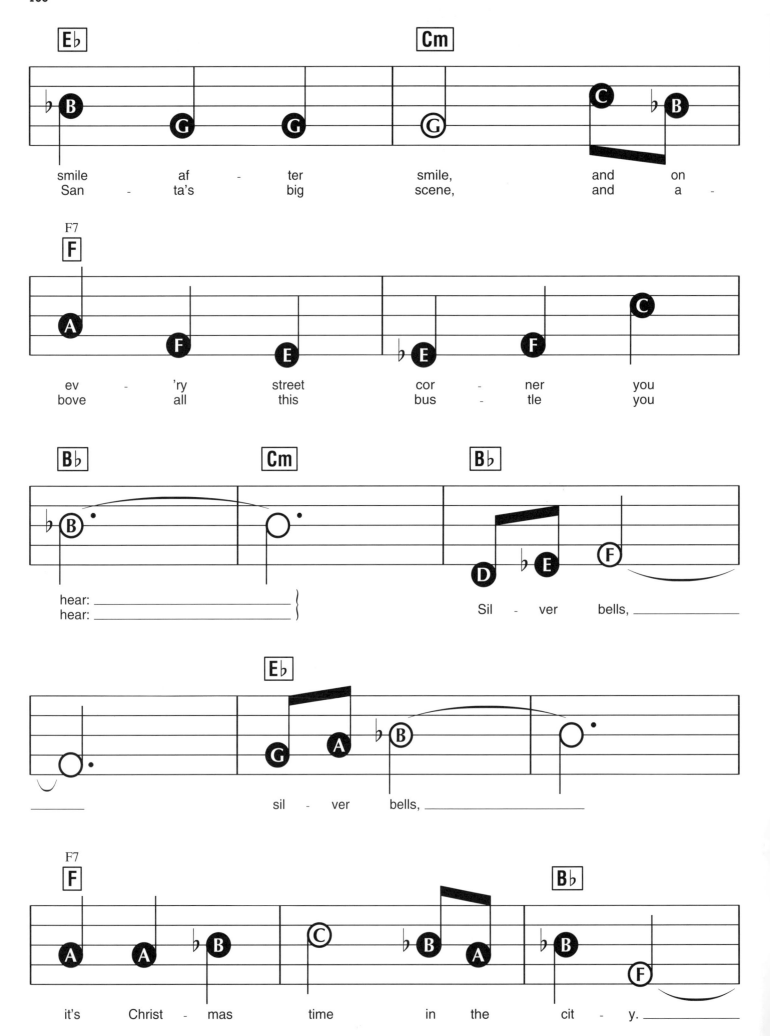

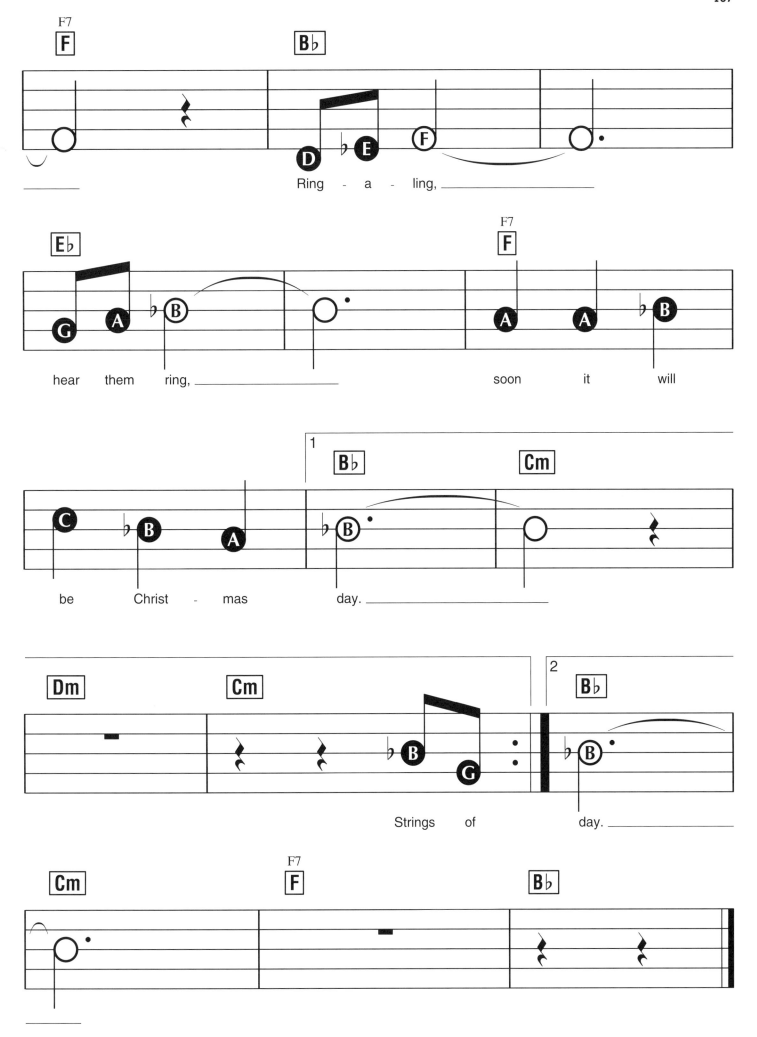

Suzy Snowflake

Registration 8
Rhythm: Fox Trot or Swing

Words and Music by Sid Tepper
and Roy Bennett

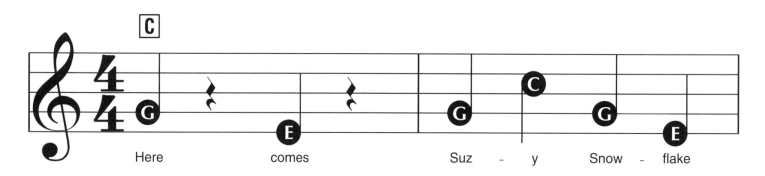

Here comes Suz-y Snow-flake

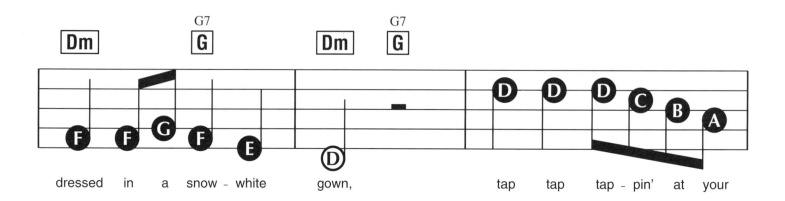

dressed in a snow-white gown, tap tap tap-pin' at your

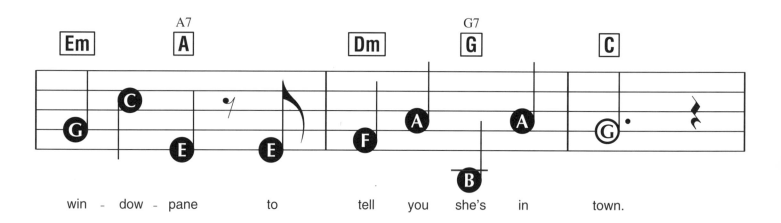

win-dow-pane to tell you she's in town.

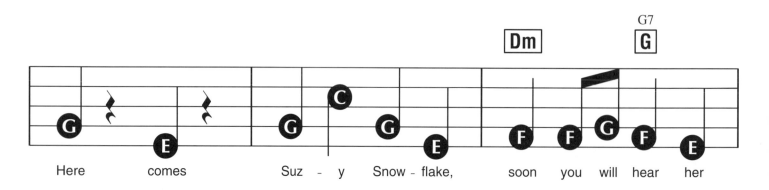

Here comes Suz-y Snow-flake, soon you will hear her

Copyright © 1951 by Chappell & Co.
Copyright Renewed
International Copyright Secured   All Rights Reserved

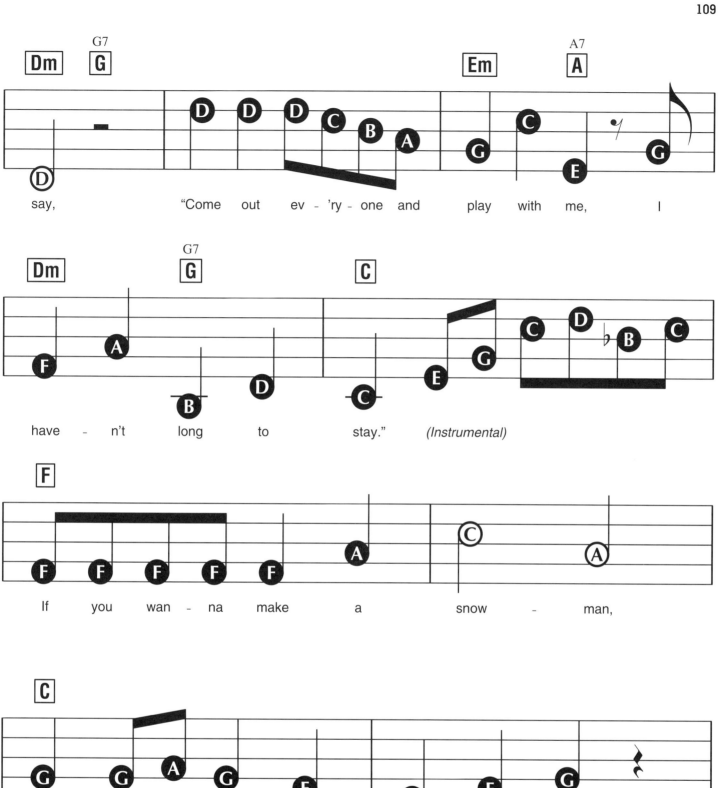
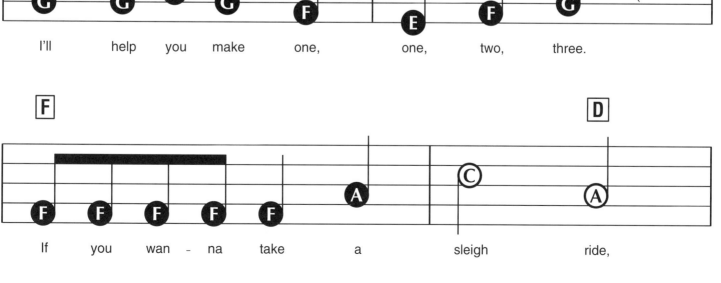

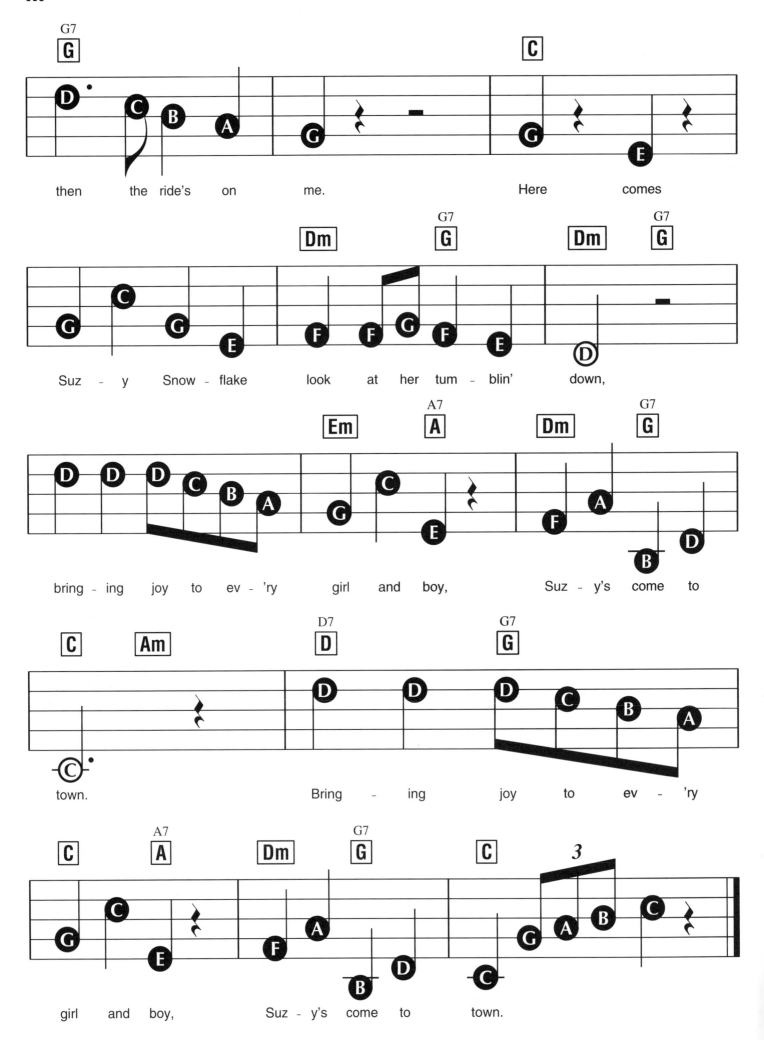

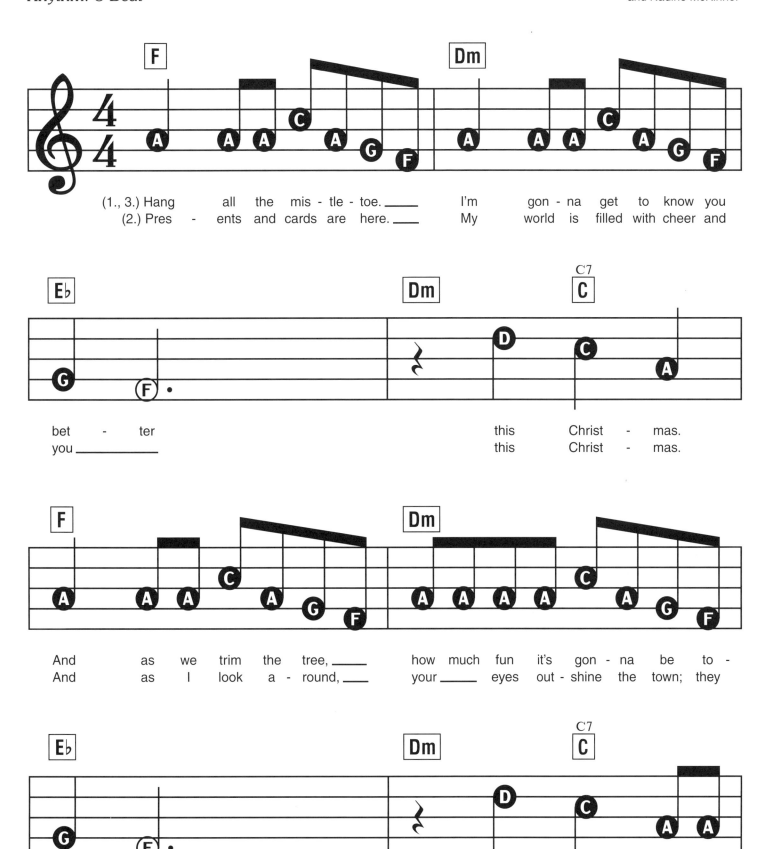

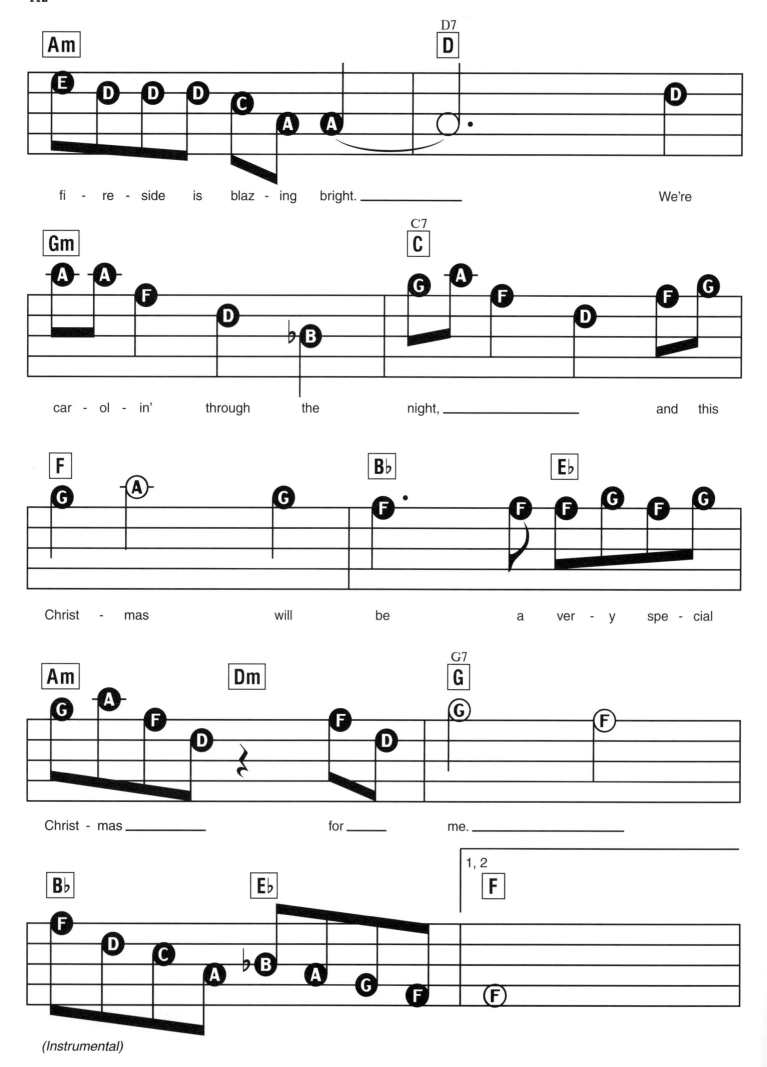

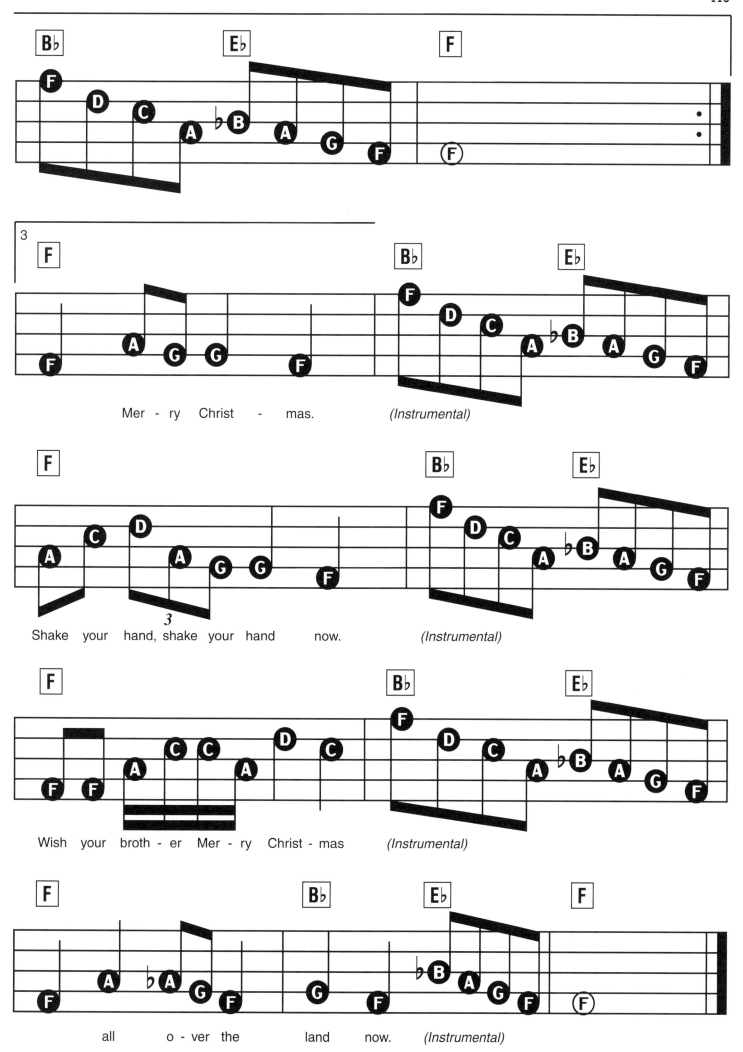

Wonderful Christmastime

Registration 3
Rhythm: Fox Trot

Words and Music by
McCartney

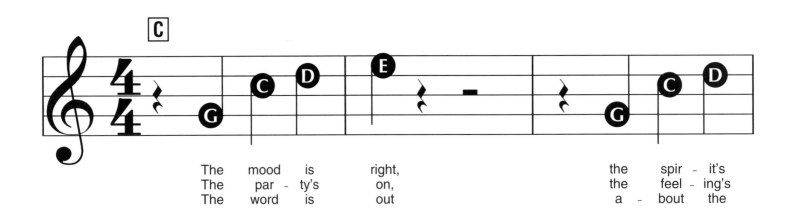

The mood is right, the spir - it's
The par - ty's on, the feel - ing's
The word is out a - bout the

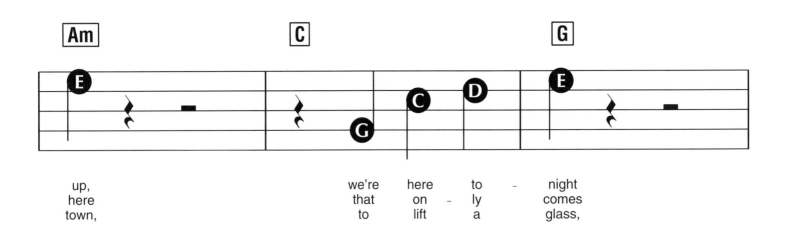

up, we're here to - night
here that on - ly comes
town, to lift a glass,

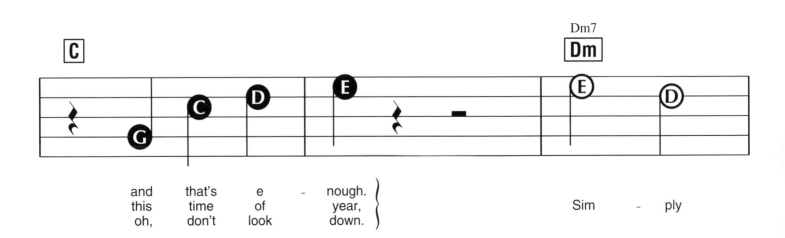

and that's e - nough.
this time of year, Sim - ply
oh, don't look down.

© 1979 MPL COMMUNICATIONS LTD.
Administered by MPL COMMUNICATIONS, INC.
All Rights Reserved

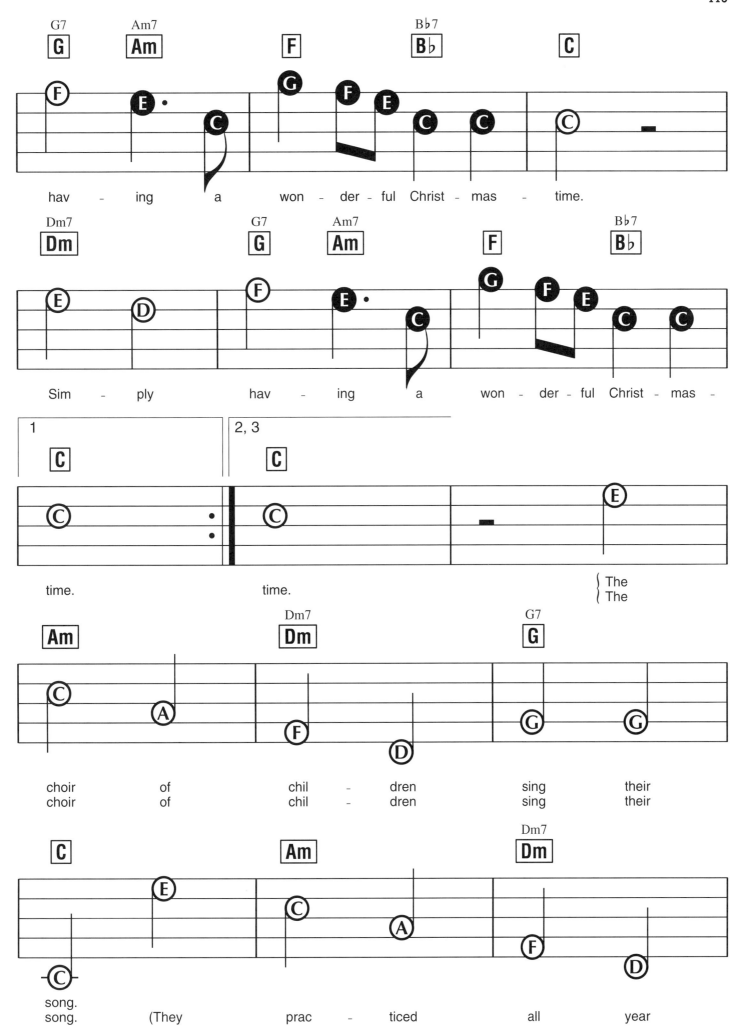

116

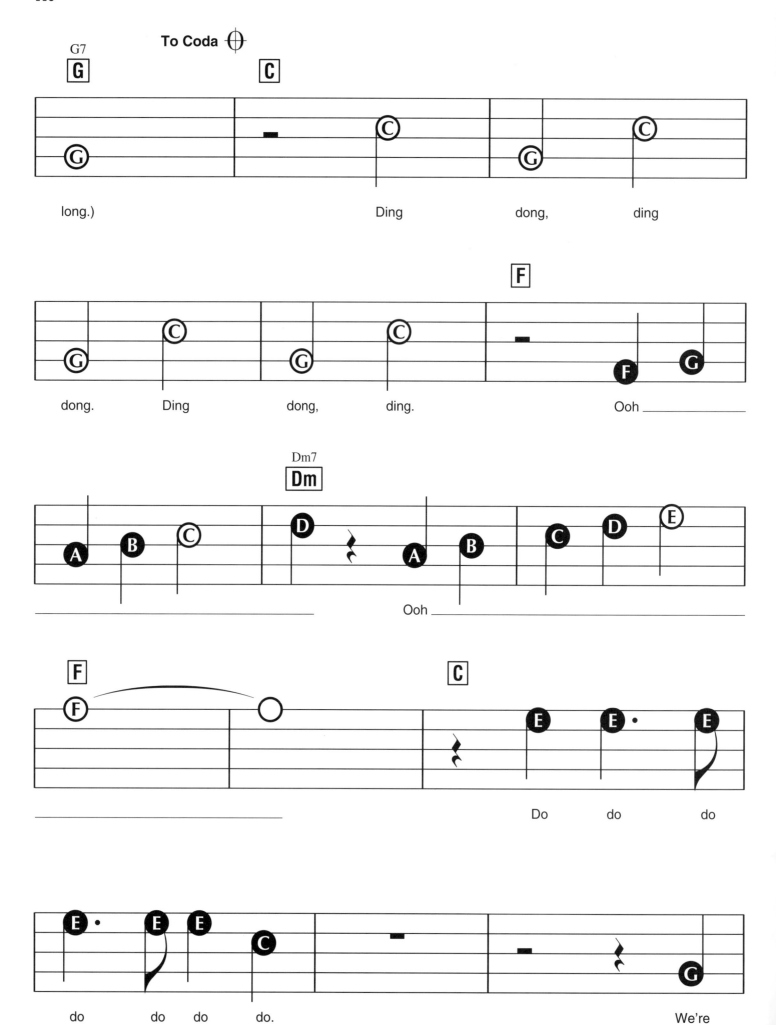

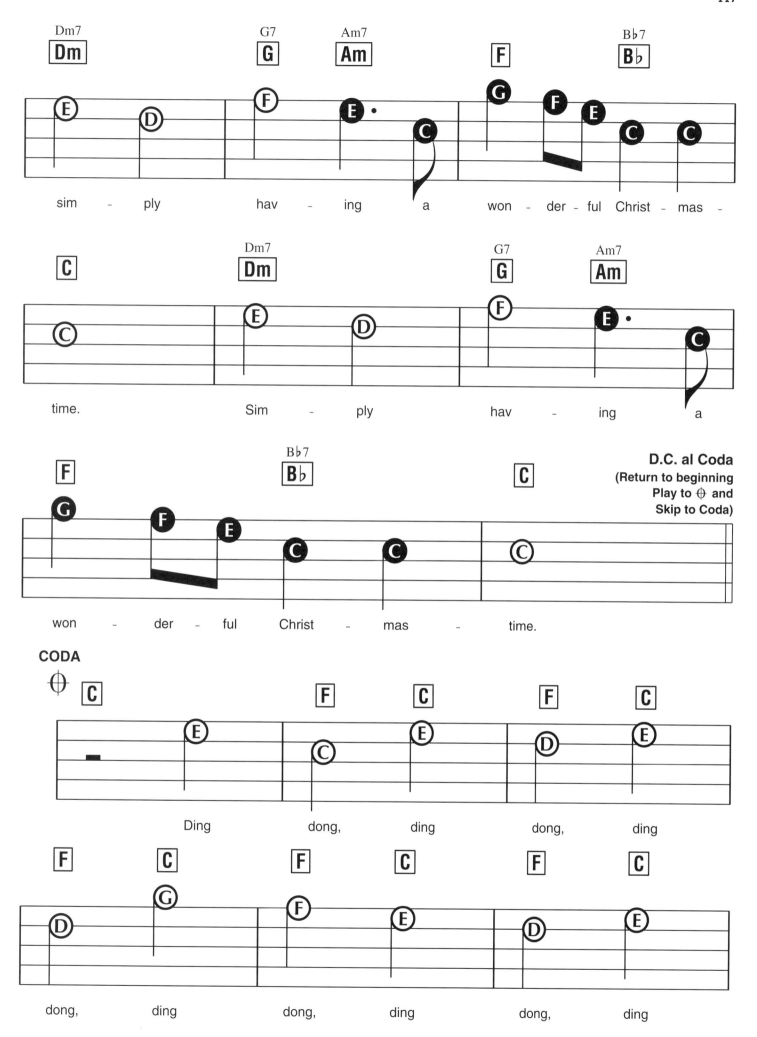

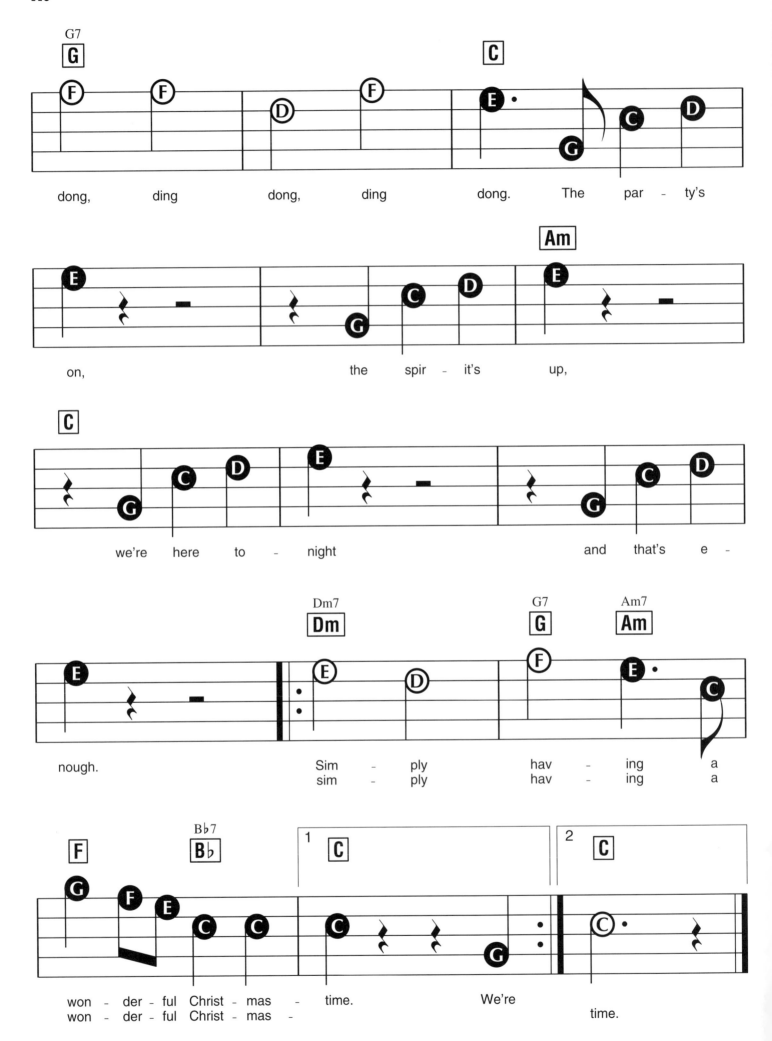

Registration Guide

- Match the Registration number on the song to the corresponding numbered category below. Select and activate an instrumental sound available on your instrument.
- Choose an automatic rhythm appropriate to the mood and style of the song. (Consult your Owner's Guide for proper operation of automatic rhythm features.)
- Adjust the tempo and volume controls to comfortable settings.

Registration

1	Mellow	Flutes, Clarinet, Oboe, Flugel Horn, Trombone, French Horn, Organ Flutes
2	Ensemble	Brass Section, Sax Section, Wind Ensemble, Full Organ, Theater Organ
3	Strings	Violin, Viola, Cello, Fiddle, String Ensemble, Pizzicato, Organ Strings
4	Guitars	Acoustic/Electric Guitars, Banjo, Mandolin, Dulcimer, Ukulele, Hawaiian Guitar
5	Mallets	Vibraphone, Marimba, Xylophone, Steel Drums, Bells, Celesta, Chimes
6	Liturgical	Pipe Organ, Hand Bells, Vocal Ensemble, Choir, Organ Flutes
7	Bright	Saxophones, Trumpet, Mute Trumpet, Synth Leads, Jazz/Gospel Organs
8	Piano	Piano, Electric Piano, Honky Tonk Piano, Harpsichord, Clavi
9	Novelty	Melodic Percussion, Wah Trumpet, Synth, Whistle, Kazoo, Perc. Organ
10	Bellows	Accordion, French Accordion, Mussette, Harmonica, Pump Organ, Bagpipes